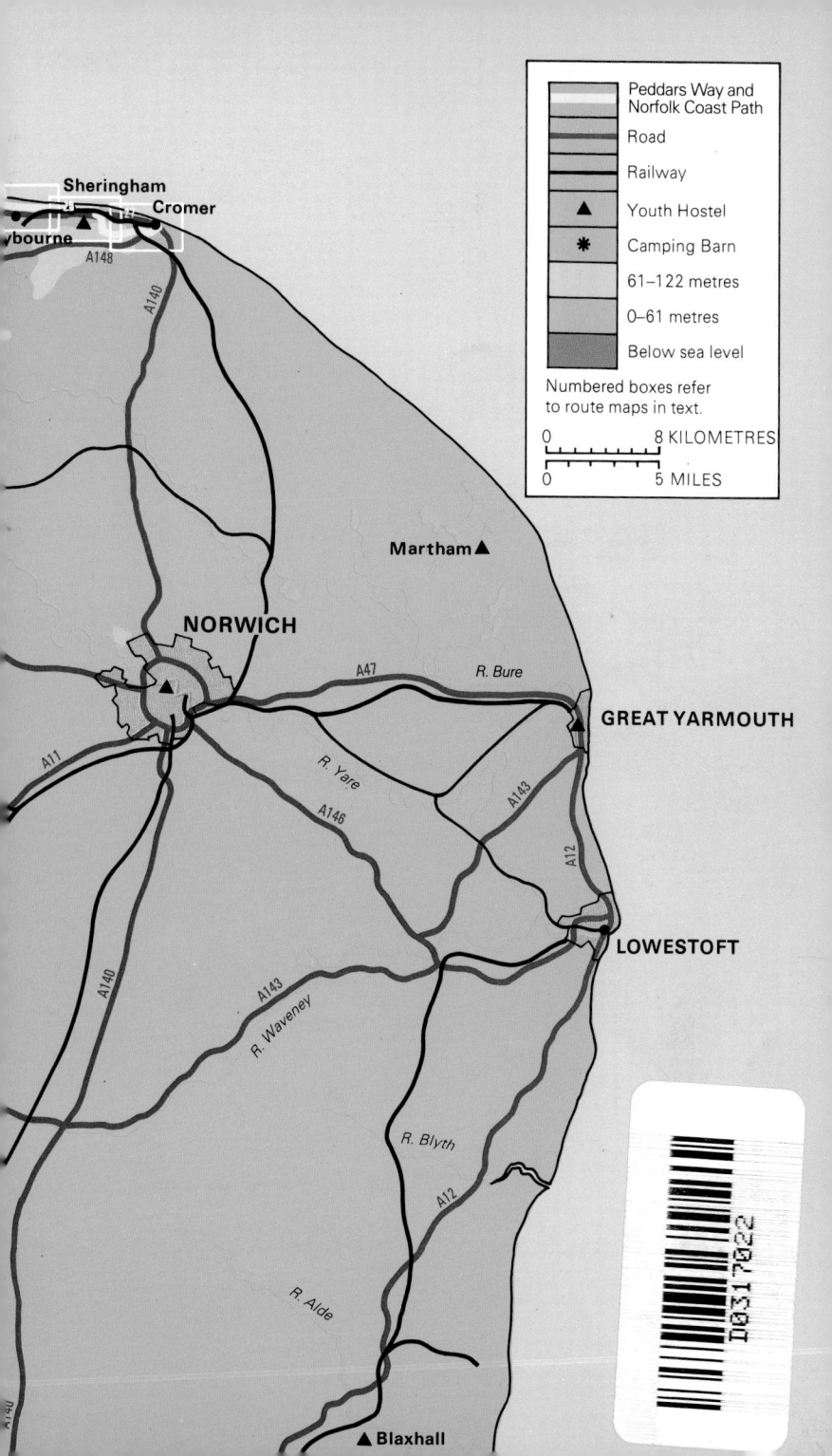

Sheringham

Cromer

ybourne

A148

A140

Peddars Way and
Norfolk Coast Path

Road

Railway

▲ Youth Hostel

✳ Camping Barn

61–122 metres

0–61 metres

Below sea level

Numbered boxes refer
to route maps in text.

0   8 KILOMETRES

0   5 MILES

Martham ▲

NORWICH ▲

A47   R. Bure

GREAT YARMOUTH

A11

R. Yare

A143

A146

A12

LOWESTOFT

A140

A143

R. Waveney

R. Blyth

A12

R. Alde

▲ Blaxhall

Acknowledgements

Many individuals helped in the preparation of this guide book, and my special thanks go to members of the staff of the Countryside Commission; to Graham King and Alan Scowen, Moria Warland, Graham White and Co., George and Jean le Surf and other members of the Peddars Way Association, Peter Lambley and John Goldsmith, Tony Gregory and Edwin J. Rose, Robin Brown, Michael Seago, my family, and to innumerable walking companions.

Any errors are mine.

Bruce Robinson

Key to cover illustrations:
1: Kestrel   2: Black-headed gulls   3: Carrion crow   4: Chaffinch
5: Rook   6: Partridge   7: Small white   8: Gatekeeper   9: Bank vole
10: Hawthorn   11: Field Poppy   12: Ox-eye daisy   13: Field scabious
14: Germander speedwell   15: Bladder campion   16: Buttercup   17: Rosebay willowherb

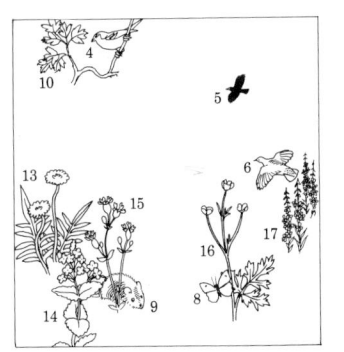

The Peddars Way and Norfolk Coast Path

Bruce Robinson

Long distance route guide No 13

London: Her Majesty's Stationery Office 1986

Published for the Countryside Commission

Front Cover: Castle Acre Priory

Back Cover: The North Norfolk Coast, near Burnham Overy Staithe

Pages x–xi The Peddars Way near Fring

The maps in this guide are extracts from Ordnance Survey 1:25,000 maps sheet nos.
TF 62/72, 63/73, 71, 74, 80, 81, 82, 84, 94, TG 04, 14, TL 89/99, 98. (The maps used are the most
up-to-date at the time of publication.)

Drawings:
Louis Mackay

Photographs: John Tyler

Long distance route guides published for the Countryside
Commission by HMSO:

The Pennine Way, by Tom Stephenson: 120 pages, £3.95 net
The Cleveland Way, by Alan Falconer: Out of print
The Pembrokeshire Coast Path, by John H. Barrett: 124
pages, £3.95 net
Offa's Dyke Path, by John B. Jones: 124 pages, £3.95 net
Cornwall Coast Path, by Edward C. Pyatt: 120 pages,
£3.95 net
The Ridgeway Path, by Seán Jennett: 120 pages, £3.95 net
South Downs Way, by Seán Jennett: 120 pages, £4.95 net
Dorset Coast Path, by Brian Jackman: 120 pages, £3.95 net
South Devon Coast Path, by Brian Le Messurier: 120
pages, £3.95 net
Somerset and North Devon Coast Path, by Clive
Gunnell: 120 pages, £3.95 net
The North Downs Way, by Denis Herbstein: 156 pages,
£3.95 net
The Wolds Way, by Roger Ratcliffe: 124 pages, £3.95 net

Government Bookshops:
49 High Holborn, London WC1V 6HB
13a Castle Street, Edinburgh EH2 3AR
Princess Street, Manchester M60 8AS
Southey House, Wine Street, Bristol BS1 2BQ
258 Broad Street, Birmingham B1 2HE
80 Chichester Street, Belfast BT1 4JY

Government publications are also available through booksellers

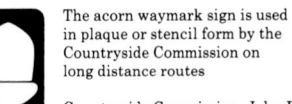

The acorn waymark sign is used
in plaque or stencil form by the
Countryside Commission on
long distance routes

Countryside Commission, John Dower House, Crescent Place,
Cheltenham, Glos. GL50 3RA

Prepared for the Countryside Commission by the Central Office of Information.
Printed in the UK for HMSO
ISBN 0 11 701191 6   Dd 718138   C250   COCO J0002 NJ

Contents

	page
Introduction	1
Some advice	3
Landscape aspects	11
Wildlife and nature reserves	22
History of the Peddars Way	33
Knettishall to Merton	41
Merton to Castle Acre	53
Castle Acre to Holme-next-the-Sea	65
Hunstanton to Brancaster	79
Brancaster to Wells-next-the-Sea	91
Wells-next-the-Sea to Cley-next-the-Sea	105
Cley-next-the-Sea to Cromer	115
Additional walks	126
Nearby places of interest	129
Accommodation	137
Useful addresses	139
Reading list	143
Countryside Access Charter	144

Maps of route

Knettishall to Merton	48–51
Merton to Castle Acre	60–63
Castle Acre to Holme-next-the-Sea	72–77
Hunstanton to Brancaster	86–89
Brancaster to Wells-next-the-Sea	101–103
Wells-next-the-Sea to Cley-next-the-Sea	112–113
Cley-next-the-Sea to Cromer	122–125

Maps reference

PEDDARS WAY AND NORFOLK COAST PATH

━━━━━━ Footpath

━·━·━·━ Footpath with permissive use for horseriders

━━ ━━ ━━ Bridleway

═══════ Unmetalled highway

════════ Metalled highway

As some short sections of the route had not been formally agreed when this book went to press, users should follow the acorn waymarks along the route

The acorn symbol with the map number is positioned on the maps at the beginning of each section of the route, working from south to north for the Peddars Way and west to east for the Norfolk Coast Path

▲ Youth hostel

✳ Camping barn

i Tourist information centre (seasonal opening)

P Parking

Location shown in the route description by bold type

Danger. Ministry of Defence Training Area
The boundaries of the Stanford Training Area are shown by permission of the Ministry of Defence

The base maps used for the route sections of this guidebook are the latest Ordnance Survey 1:25,000 maps available at the time of preparation. Some annotations have been added to bring them more up to date

Note:- Road fillings and numbers are shown in orange on the map.

Motorway. Trunk and Main Road (Dual Carriageway)	M 4 *or* A 6(M) A 123 *or* A 123(T)
Trunk & Main Road	A 123 *or* A 123(T)
Secondary Road	*Fenced* B 2314 *Unfenced*
Road Under Construction	
Other Roads	*Good, metalled* *Poor, or unmetalled*
Footpaths	FP *Fenced* FP *Unfenced*
Railways, Multiple Track	Station Road over *Cutting* *Tunnel* FB *(Footbridge)* Sidings
,, *Single Track*	Viaduct *Level Crossing* *Embankment* *Road under*
,, *Narrow Gauge*	++++++++++++++++++++++++
Boundaries County or County Borough	━ ━ ━ ━ ━
,, ,, ,, ,, ,, ,, *with Parish*	━·━·━·━·━
,, *Parish*	· · · · · · · · ·
Pipe Line (Oil, Water)	*Pipe Line*
Electricity Transmission Lines (Pylons shown at bends and spaced conventionally)	⊗ ━ ━ ━ ━ ⊗

viii

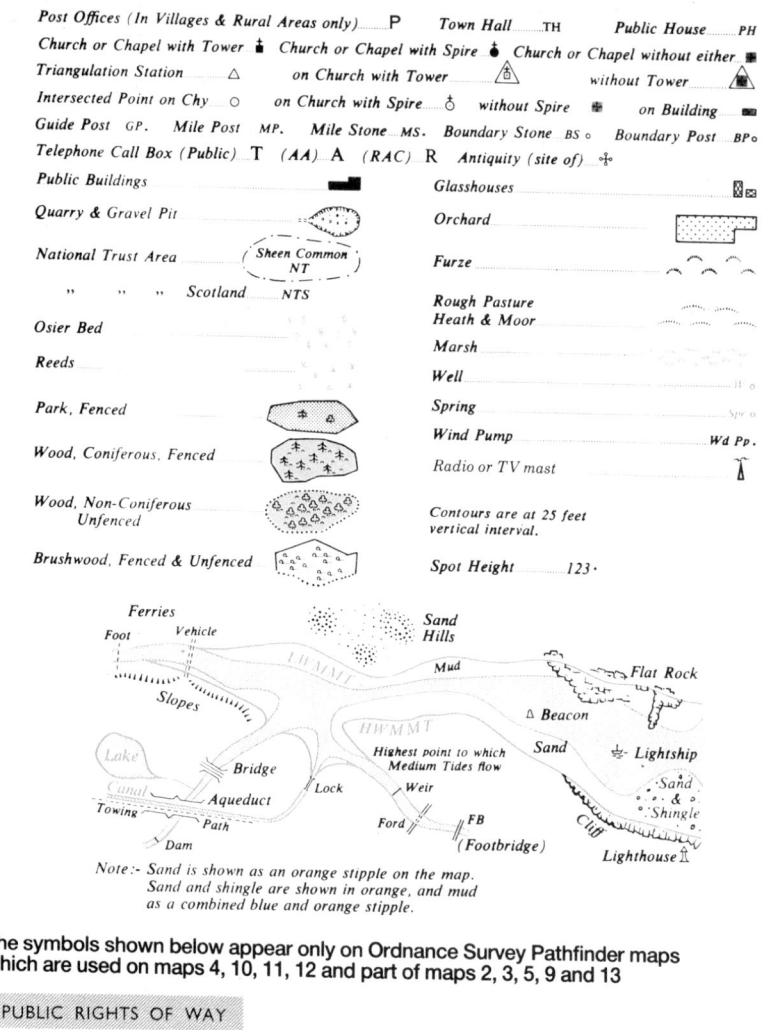

Post Offices (In Villages & Rural Areas only) P Town Hall TH Public House PH

Church or Chapel with Tower 🕈 Church or Chapel with Spire 🕈 Church or Chapel without either ■

Triangulation Station △ on Church with Tower without Tower ▲

Intersected Point on Chy ○ on Church with Spire without Spire on Building

Guide Post GP. Mile Post MP. Mile Stone MS. Boundary Stone BS ○ Boundary Post BP ○

Telephone Call Box (Public) T (AA) A (RAC) R Antiquity (site of)

Public Buildings

Quarry & Gravel Pit

National Trust Area *Sheen Common NT*

" " " Scotland NTS

Osier Bed

Reeds

Park, Fenced

Wood, Coniferous, Fenced

Wood, Non-Coniferous Unfenced

Brushwood, Fenced & Unfenced

Glasshouses

Orchard

Furze

Rough Pasture
Heath & Moor

Marsh

Well

Spring

Wind Pump Wd Pp .

Radio or TV mast

Contours are at 25 feet
vertical interval.

Spot Height 123·

Ferries

Foot Vehicle

Slopes

Lake

Canal Bridge

Aqueduct

Towing Path Lock Weir

Dam Ford FB (Footbridge)

Sand Hills

Mud

Flat Rock

HWMMT

Highest point to which
Medium Tides flow Sand

△ Beacon

Lightship

Sand & Shingle

Cliff

Lighthouse

Note:- Sand is shown as an orange stipple on the map.
Sand and shingle are shown in orange, and mud
as a combined blue and orange stipple.

The symbols shown below appear only on Ordnance Survey Pathfinder maps which are used on maps 4, 10, 11, 12 and part of maps 2, 3, 5, 9 and 13

PUBLIC RIGHTS OF WAY

- - - - - - - - - ⎫
                  ⎬ Public paths ⎰ Footpath
——— ——— ——— ⎭   ⎱ Bridleway

▬▬▬▬▬ Road used as a public path

The representation on this map of any other road, track or path is no evidence of the existence of a right of way

VEGETATION Limits of vegetation are defined by positioning of the symbols but may be delineated also by pecks or dots

Coniferous trees Scrub

Non-coniferous trees Bracken, rough grassland ⎫
                                               ⎪
Coppice In some areas bracken (⌒) and rough ⎬ Shown collectively
         grassland (⋯⋯) are shown separately ⎪ as rough grassland
                                                 ⎭ on some sheets
Orchard Heath

HEIGHTS AND ROCK FEATURES

50 · ⎫ Determined ⎰ ground survey
285 · ⎭ by   ⎱ air survey

Surface heights are to the nearest metre above
mean sea level. Heights shown close to a
triangulation pillar refer to the station height at
ground level and not necessarily to the summit

Vertical face

Loose Boulders Outcrop Scree
rock

Contours are at
5 metres
vertical interval

ix

Foreword

When the Secretary of State for the Environment agreed to the Countryside Commission's proposals to create this 13th long distance route he did so without proposing any modifications.

This, I believe, shows that the considerable number of consultations, held over a number of years prior to the Commission's submission, helped to find the right balance between providing an interesting and colourful path for walkers and finding a route that was both sensible and acceptable to the many landowners over whose land the path will cross.

The opening of the path in early 1986, less than four years after the Secretary of State's decision, will have been achieved in a shorter time than any of the preceding 12 long distance routes and illustrates very clearly the spirit of cooperation between landowners, local authorities and walkers themselves.

This cooperation has shown itself in many ways: the free offer of barns for overnight accommodation, agreements by landowners to make new sections available, the hard work and commitment of many officers in Norfolk and Suffolk County Councils, and the way in which walkers have respected the rights of landowners not to use sections of route before they are 'officially' open.

The route is in fact really two: The Norfolk Coast section is almost entirely within an area of outstanding natural beauty, and much of it falls within the heritage coast. This section is one of the richest areas in England for natural history and beauty with a great wealth of birdlife, unusual plants and spectacular views—particularly at sunrise and sunset over grazing marsh, creeks and dunes.

Peddars Way, on the other hand, is primarily a historic route passing over some of Norfolk's finest farmland but taking in sections of woodland—particularly in Breckland —country lanes and open countryside.

The whole of the path has been superbly described by Bruce Robinson who, as a local, knows every yard of it and has been able to put this description into a wider context in order to create a feel for the history, tradition and character of this part of East Anglia.

Sir Derek Barber
Chairman,
Countryside Commission

Introduction

Forty years or so ago a writer commented of the Peddars Way that it had passed into general disuse 'apparently because the place it was laid down to reach disappeared, and there was nowhere for it to go'. It was a road with no beginning and no end, and forty years ago this was substantially true. It is not strictly the case today, and in one sense at least the adopted title of the Countryside Commission's 13th long distance route—the Peddars Way and Norfolk Coast Path—betrays the reason.

Now it is two paths, joined: one ancient and historic, the other new and deliberately created. Now as one the path passes through numerous landscapes: forest and heath, modern arable, marsh and dune, cliff and village. Once again the Peddars Way does have somewhere to go.

In general detail the paths offer a 150-kilometre (93-mile) long distance route (LDR) for walkers but with sections of bridleway and quiet roads and tracks which can be used by cyclists and horseriders. It embraces a Roman road—built shortly after the tribal revolt of AD 61 led by Boudica, queen of the Iceni—country lanes, established footpaths and specially created public rights of way.

The Peddars Way runs from the Suffolk border along the north-west Norfolk ridge and continues as the Norfolk Coast Path through north Norfolk's heritage coast within an officially designated area of outstanding natural beauty. The phases are distinctive, ranging from Breckland landscapes in the south to the Goodsands of north-west Norfolk, and the marshes, beaches and cliffs of the coastline. It also passes close to or crosses fertile agricultural land and many internationally recognised wildlife reserves.

This guide is an attempt to add to your enjoyment of this gentle, fragile and varied route. Management works, of course, have been kept to a minimum, but carefully designed boardwalks, footbridges across rivers and streams, stiles and waymarks have been provided to ease your way.

There were few aids available along the Peddars Way the first time I encountered it over a decade ago. Then it was little more than a quiet rural byway remembered by many but

1

visited by very few. One or two sections of track on existing rights of way were so little used that at the height of summer the walker faced the clinging demands of waist-high vegetation and the perils of trailing brambles and branches.

In fact the planning of the new long distance route was already under way.

Norfolk County Council first proposed the project in 1969 and in January, 1974, after much discussion and consultation, finally resolved to promote it. Further discussions and the examination of a possible route continued through the next few years and embraced not only the County Council and the Countryside Commission but also the National Farmers' Union, the Country Landowners' Association, the Ramblers' Association, and others.

In the late 1970s a feasibility study was undertaken on behalf of the Countryside Commission by Mr. J. F. (Willie) Wilson, a field officer employed for the purpose by Norfolk County Council. His report, the result of detailed talks and investigation, was published by the Commission in January, 1980. Sadly, 'Willie' Wilson died in 1982.

The scheme for a long distance route was finally submitted by the Countryside Commission to the Secretary of State for the Environment in August, 1981. Three months later a Peddars Way Association was launched at an inaugural meeting in Swaffham attended by more than 100 people.

In October, 1982, the Secretary of State signified his approval and detailed planning began in earnest. In December, 1983, 'Willie's Clump', a small grouping of native trees planted beside the Peddars Way near Thompson Water on a Norfolk Naturalists' Trust nature reserve, was dedicated to the memory of J.F. Wilson.

Some advice

The value of the Peddars Way and Norfolk Coast Path in an open air sense is not the physical challenge it presents (experienced walkers might classify it as moderately testing) but the subtlety of its ever changing moods. There are cliffs and gentle hills in one or two places, to be sure, but no real summits to conquer. The relatively easy going terrain, which is marginally more difficult on the coast path, offers a generally friendly face.

In some ways the variety of surfaces reflects its continually changing character: flinty or grassy paths, metalled country roads and lanes, rutted farm tracks, breezy clifftops, shingle and sandy beaches and trails by embankments and salty creeks. The LDR embraces a real feeling of history and continuity and it is this richness, this blend of experiences, which is its real delight.

The visitor will gain new insights into the patterns of life and the tranquillity of rural Norfolk.

He or she will also come to realise just how fragile some of this richness is. You cannot gaze at the battered cliffs and stout sea defences at Hunstanton, for example, without beginning to appreciate the scale of the unceasing tug-of-war between man, land, climate and sea. Again, rare habitats and species are apparently commonplace at areas such as Knettishall, East Wretham, Thompson, Blakeney Point, Cley, Scolt Head Island and Titchwell, and yet without protection these can so easily be damaged.

Peddars Way leads the walker by a number of conserved and important areas, and through a cross section of the history of forestry, agriculture and Roman Norfolk. However, the scientific accolades piled on the north-west and north Norfolk coast suggest, in some ways, an even more impressive pedigree. Here, the undeveloped coast has been defined as heritage coast, designated as an area of outstanding natural beauty, and as a Grade 1 site of special scientific interest. The coast also includes the internationally important designation of a Ramsar site, allocated by a worldwide convention on wetlands in the 1970s, and sites of geological interest such as Blakeney Point, the Runton cliffs and Scolt Head.

The complete LDR can be walked in five days if you are a 32-kilometres (20-miles) a day walker, or in six to eight days if you prefer a more leisurely pace. By taking time out at Castle Acre or another place on or near the route it can also provide a longer holiday.

There is no good or bad time of the year to walk the path. A purely personal preference is to start in the south in or about the second week of June. For some reason I feel more relaxed walking towards the sea rather than away from it, perhaps because arrival at the coast provides a feeling of fulfilment. Anyway, in early June the vegetation is new and sweet, gorse and broom bushes are usually ablaze with yellow blossom and the hawthorn hedgerows decked in white. Then again, spring and autumn bring rare migrants to the coast, so these may be the birdwatchers' preferred times.

General facilities such as shops, pubs, telephone kiosks and post offices are in reasonable supply and usually easier to find on the Coast Path than on the Peddars Way.

Food supplies should not be a major problem. No one need walk for more than a day without being able to take on stores. The longest stretch without such facilities is probably that between Castle Acre and Ringstead and even then, if the need is great, it is quite easy to divert to Great Massingham or Sedgeford.

A guide published by the Peddars Way Association gives this sort of basic information.

Well-equipped
walkers near
Shakers Furze

Equipment

Maps, including those prepared especially for this guide, do add to the enjoyment. The Ordnance Survey's 1:50,000 Landranger sheets 144, 132, and 133 cover the route and provide an introduction to the surrounding countryside. If you require more intensive coverage, then the 1:25,000 first and second series supply fascinating detail. You do need rather a large number, though, and the sheets are expensive.

Choice of equipment is a personal matter, and the experienced backpacker will have evolved his own system and sorted out his preferences and dislikes. A few general points may be useful.

Given good (meaning dry) weather there is no reason why the walk could not be completed in strong, comfortable shoes. There are other circumstances which suggest this cannot be recommended, though. Sections of the LDR can become very wet, even during the summer. Footwear can also become soaked in areas where the track is muddy or the undergrowth long. A heavy dew on a hot summer's morning can be surprisingly damp. Other sections, particularly those incorporating shingle or sand, can be quite hard on footwear and on legs.

On balance, walking boots are better than shoes. But whatever you wear, be prepared for the wet.

Do not be misled by inland warmth. It can become quite sultry particularly in summer in Breckland where the plantations shut out the breeze and hold the heat, whereas on the more exposed coast it can be relatively chilly. Therefore, pack a sweater and warm clothing. The evenings may be cold, and winds off the sea can vary from the merely boisterous to the piercingly bitter.

Another point to keep in mind if backpacking is that you will meet other people and other modes of transport along the LDR. Norfolk's coastline is a popular area for holiday visitors (a point worth remembering when considering potential camp sites in summer) and some of the waymarked paths are ideal (and indeed signposted) for strollers. Again, some sections of the Peddars Way carry a variety of vehicles ranging from military lorries and Forestry Commission vans in the south, to farm tractors and lorries particularly on the stretch from Shepherd's Bush to Ringstead.

Warnings

There are few real dangers to life and limb, but several matters ought to be mentioned.

Common sense decrees that walkers should keep out of crops and fields, stick to defined paths, and not indulge in indiscriminate camping. Do not attempt to feed farm animals, and be careful not to leave debris, such as plastic bags, anywhere. Take them with you.

During spells of dry weather fire is an ever present possibility. Bracken and grass covered verges can become tinder dry, and heath fires sometimes occur in the county. Breckland and the Forestry Commission plantations are also high risk areas, and the dry months are a particularly anxious time for forest rangers.

The rules are: don't toss empty bottles into the undergrowth, never light fires, and make sure all cigarettes are properly extinguished.

As for the Stanford Practical Training Area, the Peddars Way touches only one short stretch of it. Warning signs abound and it is usually well fenced. There are two reasons why the boundaries should not be crossed. One is that live firing takes place on the ranges. Another is that the army has occupied the area for over 40 years, and it is now littered with munitions.

The coast

Swimming and coastal defences must also be mentioned, if only because Norfolk's pleasant coastline disguises some dangerous traits.

Some beaches are steeply shelved, a matter which constantly takes the unwary by surprise, and there are some very nasty undercurrents. If you see a red flag hoisted it means 'Danger, no bathing'. Do remember, though, that the flag system does not operate everywhere.

Keep a weather eye open, do not venture out to sea on unsecured dinghies or sea-beds, or swim from deserted beaches near groynes or breakwaters. And never dive off them.

Brancaster, Burnham Overy Staithe, Wells and Blakeney are tidal harbours and swimming in the channels is very dangerous when the tide is flooding or ebbing. The wreck at Brancaster is best avoided as there is a danger of being cut off by the tide.

The sands on the east side of Wells channel can also be reached on foot at low water, and here one can also become cut off by the tide. During the holiday season a horn is sounded to warn people to return to the main beach. If you are cut off by the tide here you should not attempt to cross

The coastline near Sheringham golf course

the channel. Instead, go to East Hills and wave to attract attention.

There are also paths across the marshes at Stiffkey to the foreshore and therefore the possibility of being cut off. In addition, the beaches at Cley, Salthouse and Weybourne shelve steeply and there is a strong undertow, making swimming dangerous.

If any sort of water-based emergency does arise dial 999 and ask for the coastguards. There are emergency telephones at Wells (attached to the coastguards lookout) and at Cley.

Also, a substantial part of the coastal route runs on or near sea defences which include sand-dunes and clay and shingle banks. Stay on the proper path, please. Another point to remember, particularly in the area around Weybourne and Sheringham, is that the cliffs are subject to undercutting by the sea and thus prone to erosion. The prospect of cliff falls is very real, so stay away from the edge.

In general, take note of all warning notices prominently displayed in any hazardous area.

The weather

An abundance of open space lends richness to the skies and weather of Norfolk. The area enjoys a fine quality of light and is noted for its sunrises and sunsets. Sky and cloud form an integral part of the interplay between light and landscape, particularly along the coast.

The location of East Anglia means that its climate, especially inland, is more continental than the rest of the British Isles. Annual rainfall is low, averaging between 500–600 millimetres (20–25 inches). There is little seasonal variation, though the heaviest falls often tend to come between June and October. The months between February and April–June tend to have the lowest average totals.

A number of other aspects are worth noting.

Figures for sunshine duration are generally high; there is a relatively high frequency of summer thunderstorms; East Anglia is famous for its drying and/or bracing breezes; in spring, east winds are liable to bring chilly temperatures and sometimes sea fog: and winds from between east and north are inclined to bring rain and cloudy skies.

Two forms of meteorological forecast are available by telephone. The East Anglia Weatherline recorded forecast is obtainable on Norwich (0603) 8091. A more detailed personal forecast is available (6.30 a.m. to 8 p.m.) from the Norwich Weather Centre on Norwich (0603) 660779.

Waymarks

Two general types of waymark are employed along the length of the route. At all important junctions there are waymarks which indicate either 'Peddars Way' or 'Coast Path' on plain wood fingerposts with incised lettering. Elsewhere green, yellow and white discs are used. All signs incorporate the acorn which is used to waymark all long distance routes.

Bridleways

Bridleway stretches of the LDR are waymarked by blue arrows. Riders are reminded that along the coast the sections tend to be isolated and fragmented and that a continuous route (from Hunstanton to Cromer) does not at present exist.

One continuous LDR bridleway has been specially designed. It begins near the railway line at Bridgham Heath (about 8 kilometres north-east of Thetford, on the A11) and, basically following the Peddars Way, continues across country to Holme-next-the-Sea. In several places it diverts from the LDR to take in Cockley Cley, the Fincham Drove road, Fring and Beacon Hill.

Stabling and adjacent accommodation are in short supply, but the situation is improving as further facilities are developed.

A leaflet describing this route and listing local contacts—*Peddars Way: a route for horseriders*—is obtainable from the Department of Planning and Property of Norfolk County Council (see Useful addresses).

Transport

Rail links with the two extremes of the route are stronger at the coast than they are inland. There is a good local service between Norwich and Cromer. There is no railway at Knettishall; however, there are local services on the Norwich–Ely line, and stops at Brandon, Thetford and Harling Road offer the possibility of travellers alighting here and walking to Knettishall. Thetford and Harling Road are the closest to Knettishall, but both walks take a couple of hours or so. From Brandon it is possible to walk the length of the Harling Drove to join the Peddars Way near A11 trunk road at either East Wretham (Stonebridge) or Bridgham Heath.

Not all trains stop at every station, however. As new time-tables for these pay trains operate from the middle of May each year, it is best to check with British Rail.

There are also good bus links between Norwich and Cromer with daily services by Eastern Counties Omnibus

Village post office

Company. However, ECOC does not call at Knettishall. A useful ECOC stopping place is the East Harling (Larling) crossroads request stop on the Norwich–Thetford road. From here it is possible to walk to join the path. Again, it will take an hour or two. Do not contemplate walking along the busy and dangerous A11, however. There are also ECOC services from Bury St. Edmunds to nearby Barningham and Hopton.

ECOC does link with other places on or near the LDR (eg Watton, Swaffham, Castle Acre, Harpley, Sedgeford, King's Lynn, Hunstanton, Holme, Brancaster, Wells, Sheringham), but do remember that services can be infrequent and journey times long.

ECOC's seasonal timetables start around mid-June and operate to early September. It is essential to check them before planning a walk.

Other links with Knettishall are maintained by a private bus operator, C. E. Petch (see Useful addresses), who provides a service which runs several times a week calling at Thetford, Knettishall and other places in the vicinity.

At the time of writing there are no overnight car parking facilities at Knettishall, but visitor parking is provided at the country park to the east of the southern end of the route and about five minutes' walk away. A small car park at the start of the LDR may be provided at Knettishall in the future.

Parking facilities at the eastern end of the coastal route are more plentiful. Cromer, of course, is a busy seaside resort.

Landscape aspects

Norfolk boasts the lowest high point in the country, but only someone who has never walked or cycled would say that it is flat. It is not. Truly flat landscapes exist hereabouts only in some of the valleys of the Broadland rivers to the east and in the Fens to the west. Norfolk's hills are merely of a modest scale.

Because it is relatively low-lying it is short of large dramatic features, but there are compensations in the importance of sky, the subtlety of colour, and the gentle simplicity of an immensely rich, varied and undulating landscape. Considerable forces, however, were necessary to create it.

Of the three major phases of glaciation it was the first, the Anglian, which proved the most widespread, the ice reaching as far south as the Thames Valley. The Wolstonian, from the north and west, spread almost as far, while the Devensian left the area south of the coast at Hunstanton largely unglaciated.

The general effect of all this change was the smoothing down of the chalk ridge and the depositing of wide tracts of boulder clay and gravel which covered the earlier rocks and former estuarine deposits. Drainage patterns were also altered and to a large extent the ice phases dictated the basic shape—with the exception of the coastline—of the Norfolk countryside.

Man's arrival in the region can only loosely be dated to about 400,000 BC when Norfolk, of course, was still united to the Continent. The North Sea basin, once a land of forest, swamp and freshwater pools, finally succumbed to inundation about 6400 BC (radio-carbon dating), and at several points on the north Norfolk coast, notably at Gore Point and Titchwell, the trunks and stools of ancient trees can still be seen at low tide.

Despite his evident longevity as a resident, man has nevertheless farmed the area for only 5,000 years or so. At Hurst Fen, near Mildenhall, the Neolithic inhabitants lived by cultivating emmer (a species of wheat) and barley, and possibly by keeping cattle, pigs, sheep and goats. By the emergence of the Bronze Age some fields were being

Quiet evening near Morston

ploughed while others were given over to the grazing of herds and flocks.

Today, the watershed of the east-coast rivers and the Wash rivers is still the area of heavy soil chiefly derived from boulder clay, a tract which divides the centre of Norfolk and Suffolk and which formerly supported woodland. The chalk ridge also remains a substantial element. Eight to 16 kilometres wide and over 300 metres thick in places, it may have formed a belt of relatively open country to the west of the boulder clay after the Neolithic period.

One of the most fascinating historic and present-day landscapes is **Breckland**, a name which refers in general to flint strewn fields, open heaths and short vegetation, and which was first coined in 1894 by the Thetford historian, W.G. Clarke.

After the Norman Conquest what had been a prosperous agricultural area gradually declined as more fertile lands were developed elsewhere. By the 17th century the region was mainly used for grazing sheep. At the same time a rapid increase in the rabbit population led to the destruction of vegetation to such an extent that it became a virtual desert, an open bracken-filled landscape subject to sand and dust storms.

Following enclosure acts of the early 1800s belts of trees and hedgerows were planted in an attempt to reduce erosion, but a depressed farming economy led to the impoverishment of many estates. Much of the land reverted to rabbit infested heath. There was considerable poverty in Breckland at this time, and many farmers had recourse to rabbit farming, the pelts finding a market in fur felt factories in Brandon and the carcasses in London.

Red
squirrel

Oak
(Pedunculate)

Jay

Red
deer

Crossbill

Corsican
pine

Silver
birch

Magpie

Fallow
deer

Hawfinch

Nightjar

Land quality and value slowly deteriorated, and it was this availability of cheap land, coupled with increased demand for timber during and after the First World War, which first brought the **Forestry Commission** into the area. The beginnings of Thetford Forest date from 1922 when the first area near Swaffham was acquired. By 1937 the majority of the land was afforested.

Today, **Thetford Forest** is the largest lowland forest in the country and the Commission's premier pine forest. Many of the original Scots pine plantations are now replanted with Corsican pine, which produces a larger volume and matures earlier.

Incidentally, one of the few charcoal burners in the locality can sometimes be glimpsed from the train in a forest clearing on the north side of the railway line not far from Brandon timber depot.

Military influence

The influence of the military and its main Norfolk battleground, the Stanford Practical Training Area, better known as the **Battle Area**, has been considerable. A generation of Breckland folk still harbour sadness over the way their homes were taken. Now, more than 40 years after the evacuation and despite an annual through-put of about 80,000 troops, it is the largest unofficial nature reserve in the county and one of the most beautiful parts of Norfolk. Alas, it is still firmly closed to the general public.

The LDR touches one corner of the Battle Area but its presence, announced in the Thompson Water area by fences and notices, extends much further than that. In all the Battle Area amounts to about 17,500 acres, of which some 2,000 acres are tenant-farmed. Some 10,000 sheep also graze the area, evidently unconcerned by all the activity.

Early in the Second World War the heaths, estates and forests of Breckland provided a ready-made troop training area, and there were many camps in the vicinity. As far as the army was concerned, however, the missing ingredients were freedom of movement and facilities for live firing. Therefore in June, 1942, it was announced that 'several' East Anglian villages were to be evacuated and the following month residents were moved to temporary accommodation. Young and old, furniture and farms, livestock and homes departed in a procession of vans, tractors, horse-drawn carts and open lorries. Fruit was left on the trees and crops in the fields.

The War Department took, in addition to land, the small

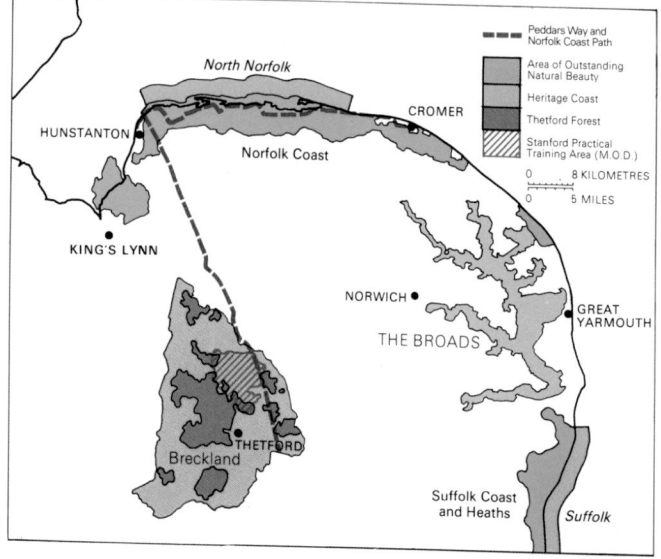

Designated areas

villages of West Tofts, Stanford and Tottington, and the tiny hamlets of Langford and Sturston. In all it embraced some 150 houses and cottages, three schools, two public-houses and 54 kilometres (34 miles) of public highway. The procession of evacuees had numbered 1,000 people.

The Battle Area is vital, the military says, to its training programmes. They certainly make full use of it and cannot be accused of destroying it. Although most of the houses have gone, their foundations are marked by sad piles of rubble; but that happened 40 years ago. The roads and churches remain, safe and shuttered and empty, and clumps of fruit trees and flowers sometimes indicate former kitchen gardens. It is a largely deserted ghostland.

Today, Breckland as a whole offers a landscape of dry, marginal land, looming blocks of pine plantations, and lines of ancient Scots pines embroidering the edges of stony fields; wide skies and light of a special and particular clarity.

Agrarian revolution

Sheep profoundly influenced the East Anglian region. In Norfolk, Flemish weavers settled at Worstead (a name still enshrined in the textile industry) and then in Norwich shortly after the Norman Conquest.

Flocks were introduced on a considerable scale in the 15th and 17th centuries, during which period the economies of many villages collapsed because of social change, industrial pressure, the ambition of landowners, sickness, and exhaus-

15

tion of the soil. Below the surface of Norfolk's landscape lie the remains of dozens of deserted villages.

The Agrarian Revolution—its influence being equally as great if not greater than the Industrial Revolution—began in Norfolk, emerging largely through the ideas of **Viscount 'Turnip' Townshend**, of Raynham Hall, and the enthusiasm of **Thomas Coke** (pronounced Cook) of Holkham.

At the beginning of the 18th century much land was still being farmed in open fields and it was Coke who adopted the idea of the 'Norfolk four-course crop rotation', applied it to his home farms and imposed it on his tenants.

The method of rotation gave greater yields and reduced pests and disease, but the land had to be enclosed to keep livestock from the crops. Hedges and trees were planted and the open fields swept away in a wave of enclosures. Between about 1750 and 1850 the countryside was remodelled and much of the rural pattern we see today established.

One current and comparatively small crop worthy of mention is mustard, which is constantly confused with oil-seed rape, though it has the broader leaf. Jeremiah Colman

Yellow-hammer

Elder

Hogweed

Pheasant

Tufted vetch

Stoat

Cow parsley

Dog rose

Harvest operation

began milling mustard in a watermill at Stoke Holy Cross in 1814, and there are now nearly 6,000 acres of it grown annually, all of it in Essex, Norfolk, Suffolk, Cambridgeshire, Lincolnshire and South Humberside. Cole-seed (as the variety of rape was once known) was crushed to produce colza-oil for burning in lamps before the advent of paraffin, the residue seed being used for manuring the land and for cattle cake. Rape-seed oil is now used for, among other things, margarine and lubricating oil.

Norfolk is one of the best husbanded areas of farmland in the country, rich soils growing fine crops of wheat and barley. There is no denying, either, the visual attraction of a crowded palette of farmland colours often enhanced by red pantiled barns and, in some parts, the use of flint, gingery brown carstone and clunch (compressed chalk) in the vernacular buildings.

Social changes

Beneath the surface of the colours and textures, however, the social changes of the last hundred years have been dramatic.

The coming of the railways in the mid-19th century gave impetus to the de-population of the rural areas as the availability of travel and the lure of growing industries attracted increasing numbers to the larger centres. There was a further profound shift after the Second World War when increasing farm mechanisation and larger fieldscapes, and an explosion in the number of car owners, caused the balance to tilt even further away from the rural communities.

17

For many small towns and villages the effects, and those of two stringent economic measures of the last decade or so, have proved far-reaching if not fatal. Many have lost schools and shops and pubs and are now divorced from rail and bus services. Some of the villages stand like many of Norfolk's churches, isolated in lonely landscapes.

But that is not all of the story, for part of the trend is now being reversed. The county's population—currently around 700,000—is increasing by about 4,000 a year, most of them filtering through to the rural areas. The villages, in turn, are trying to meet the challenge by constructing frameworks of self-help groups and community bus schemes.

Two significant factors stand out. This dramatic population rise is 'retirement-led' rather than 'industry-led', which is leading to fears of an age-structure heavily weighted by the elderly. Another factor, revealed in the 1981 Census, is that an unusually high 68 per cent of Norfolk households have access to one or more cars. This, of course, in an area with a comparatively low level of income.

Norfolk's new villagers tend to be those able to afford second homes, commuters (to London, Norwich or nearby towns) and, more particularly, the retired.

Maritime history
The influence of the sea and maritime trade has also been profound. A State paper of 1565 relating to customs and ports, for example, includes a surprising array of names still on today's maps, among them, and in addition to King's Lynn, the head port: Heacham, Hunstanton, Thornham, Burnham, Brancaster, Wells, Blakeney, Wiveton, Cley, Salthouse, Weybourne, Sheringham, Cromer and so on.

What is remarkable about the list is the number of places now largely cut off from the sea. Nevertheless, this was once one of England's busiest coastlines, the sometimes distant trade links finally proving susceptible, it seems, to the coming of railways, coastal erosion and silting, and to marsh drainage.

A further indication of maritime links is the fact that **Vice-Admiral Viscount Nelson** ('Nelson of Trafalgar') was born at Burnham Thorpe and was educated and spent his early years in Norfolk. 'I am myself,' he said at Great Yarmouth in 1800 on his return to England after the Battle of the Nile, 'a Norfolk man, and glory in being so.'

Beyond King's Lynn the hem of the Wash salt-marsh tapers away at Hunstanton, and the cliffs appear. Eastwards, the salt-marshes begin again, and from then on the coastline develops into a glorious series of natural and man-made zones, each clearly recognisable and quite distinctive. Seaward of many villages—some of them former ports—lie creeks, bands of reclaimed and unreclaimed marsh, and grazing areas criss-crossed by networks of drainage channels. An ecological wonderland divided from the sea by banks, dunes and spits.

Heritage Coast

Norfolk's defined heritage coast stretches from Holme to Salthouse. The salt-marshes are appreciated because of their size, wildness, wildlife, creeks and simple colours which together form patterns which cannot fail to impress. The dunes and flats are the most impressive coastal feature, and the stretch between Gun Hill and Holkham Gap is perhaps the most compelling sight on the coast, simply because of its magnitude. The shingle ridges and spits are constantly being modified by tide and current, and graphically show the power and influence of sea and wind.

These landscapes always have been remote and isolated and they appeal to those who can surmount this insularity. Once accepted they provide a feeling of peace and tranquillity through a unique blend of sound, light, colour and movement.

Working environment

The modern demands of agriculture and its associated economics are such that conflict between landowner and

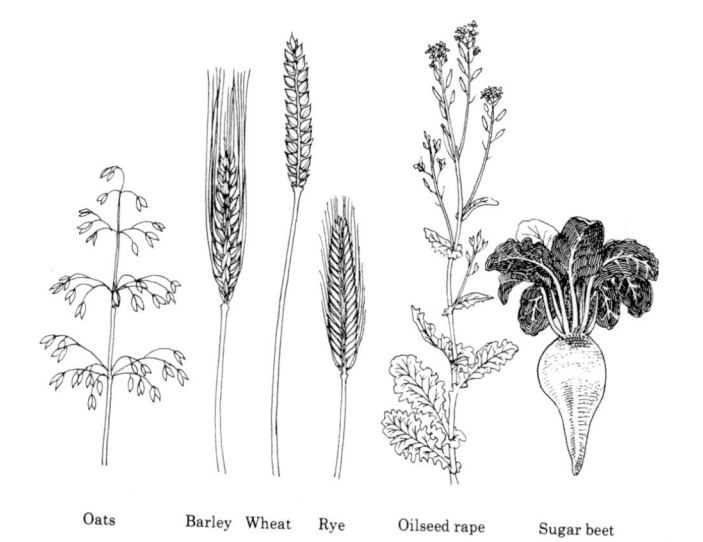

Oats   Barley   Wheat   Rye   Oilseed rape   Sugar beet

visitor, urban sprawl and rural tradition, farmer, planner, walker and environmentalist, is inevitable.

Some of the fears are not unreasonable. Crops, stock, buildings and machinery are vulnerable, and landowners and farmers have a legitimate concern over trespassers. For these reasons walkers need to remember they are passing through a working environment.

Conversely, the other side of the argument also has merit. Modern farming has much to answer for in reducing landscape value and conservation interest. At last the rate of general hedgerow decline seems to be slowing but among other things it is now a growing loss of permanent grassland which is giving cause for concern. In general, habitat losses since the last war are thought to be much heavier than at first suspected.

Conservation

Ironically, or perhaps inevitably, Norfolk has led the way in the matter of conservation. **The Norfolk Naturalists' Trust**, founded in 1926 for the purpose of acquiring properties in the county requiring protection as nature reserves, and holding them in perpetuity, was the first county-based voluntary nature conservation organisation in Britain. Today, the Trust has responsibility for over 35 properties covering some 2,425 hectares (6,000 acres) in representative parts of the county, including Broadland, Breckland and along the coast.

South
Pickenham post
office

Boats on the
beach at Cromer

It is interesting to note that protected areas including nature and bird reserves, Thetford Forest, sites of special scientific interest, and certain Broads areas, represent about five per cent of the county of Norfolk; or $1\frac{1}{2}$ per cent measured in terms of land actually managed for wildlife.

If I were forced to nominate a preference among all this richness I would linger over St. Edmund's Point atop Hunstanton cliffs, where you can stand in the wind and gaze towards the Lincolnshire coast across the Wash. I would certainly contemplate dear old Cromer, of lifeboat, crab, and Poppyland fame; the dells and dales of Roman Camp, hidden in the hills behind the Runtons; the wild isolation of Gore Point; and the dunes and expanse of Holkham Bay. In the end, though, I would vote for a wider area.

Breckland has an initial harshness about it. Bracken invades the open spaces. The plantations seem dark and still and uniform. Flinty stones glint in dusty fields, and horizons are marked not by gentle hedgerows but by gnarled and twisted pines. This is only the half of it, though. Breckland also has a smell, colour, history and atmosphere all of its own.

It is a very personal thing, but travelling towards the Brecks I always feel as though I am going home.

Wildlife and nature reserves

The considerable variety of types of landscape, and in consequence the variety of the flora and fauna, lends a particular richness to the walk.

Inland, the heaths and forests of Breckland and the agricultural 'uplands' of west Norfolk are complemented, along the coast, by a chain of important reserves stretching some 40 kilometres from Holme to Salthouse. Here, amid some of the largest salt-marshes in Britain, classic studies have been undertaken on the formation of shingle, sand-dunes and marsh systems.

A general temperate climate and lower than average rainfall, particularly in Breckland, contribute in no small measure to all this variety. There are problems, though. Winds from the north and east and off the sea can have a razor-cutting edge; and low rainfall coupled with drying winds and light soils means that irrigation of agricultural fields often becomes essential.

External circumstances have also played an important role, and it is interesting to note that of the 52 species of mammal so far recorded in Norfolk some 20 per cent are not native and have been introduced.

In comparatively recent years introduced species which have adapted are the troublesome coypu—which first appeared in nutria farms in the 1920s and 1930s and later escaped to the wild—and the grey squirrel. In 1962, when they peaked at about 200,000, Norfolk could claim to have the largest coypu population in the world! Now they are hunted regularly and professionally. As for the grey squirrel, it has spread all over the county leaving the red squirrel in decline in small scattered pockets and at a level which suggests it could shortly become extinct.

Two landmarks have seen a serious decline in recent years—the elm, ravaged by Dutch elm disease, and the oak. Vast numbers of oaks have matured and died, or are dying. Stag-headed oaks and dead elms are familiar sights. Some years ago Norfolk County Council and others embarked on a substantial programme of tree planting in an attempt to plug gaps in the face of losses of these and other species.

Brettenham
Heath

Knettishall, in the south, is an unusual area for a number of reasons, the first being that although it is close to the Little Ouse river and the forest plantations, it also embraces remnants of Breckland heath and a mix of heather and grass. It is a popular and much visited 180-acre country park, with a surface mosaic which incorporates chalk underlying sand and the more acidic conditions which encourage heather.

This unusual mix in what is in effect a pleasant and shallow river valley is reflected in its plant life, which includes harebell, tormentil, dropwort and carline thistle.

Heathland

Some of the Breckland heaths attract the nightjar and lapwing, the cinnabar moth and the orange-tip butterfly. One of the newer national nature reserves is **Brettenham Heath**, to the west of the Peddars Way and south of the A11 trunk road. Leased by the Nature Conservancy Council from Shadwell Estate Co., it represents one of the largest blocks of heath left in Breckland. It embraces areas of heather and grass, others of invading bracken, birch and hawthorn, and supports a wide variety of birdlife. Brettenham Heath is not, however, open to the public.

Lapwing

Scots pine

Roe hind

Gorse

Rosebay
willowherb

Golden
pheasant

Red-backed
shrike

Bracken

Stone curlew

Stonechat

Harebell

Green
hairstreak

Heather

Grass snake

Tormentil

East Wretham, a nature reserve covering some 145 hectares (360 acres) of heath and woodland, and which may be visited, has been in the care of the Norfolk Naturalists' Trust since 1938. It includes two well known Breckland meres, Lang Mere and Ring Mere, and adjoining woodland. Unusually, the water level of Breck meres is determined by the water table in the underlying chalk and not by rainfall and run-off.

This is typical Breck country which in other areas has been altered by afforestation, and the sandy soil supports continental plants unusual in England. The reserve is also known for the variety of its birds which include hawfinch, crossbill and woodpecker. Red and roe deer frequent the area, and there is a continual war against scrub, particularly in those areas where the sheep do not graze.

Thompson Common is one of the Norfolk Naturalists' Trust's more recent acquisitions. **Thompson Water**, a secluded lake which is now part of the reserve, is artificial, and was latterly used as a fishery. The Common itself has a rich variety of wildlife and plantlife, and is particularly known for its pingos, or circular indentations, which support a good growth of water plants.

Pingos relate to the freeze-thaw periods of the Devensian glaciation and were originally formed by the freezing water, perhaps at the top of groundwater springs. The repeated addition of ice caused a dome of the surface gravels. When the ice melted the centre of the pingo subsided to form a hollow, or pond. Sediment which had flowed off was left as an encircling rampart.

Two public trails (Common and Watering) will shortly be waymarked, and there will be information boards and car parks. **Thetford Forest** is essentially a working area, but the Forestry Commission has done much in recent years to turn it into a major place of recreation, too. There are footpaths, car parks and picnic areas, and yet the forests are so large it is usually possible to walk there and find solitude.

The plantations are clear-felled at 30–50 years, the felled area being replanted with Corsican pine seedlings grown in greenhouses at Santon Downham.

These are 'clean'—some would say sterile—woods in a sense that they tend to be uniform in terms of trees (other than the amenity belts) and ground cover. Nevertheless, diversity does exist. Between 70 and 80 bird species nest in the forest and many more are known to visit the area.

A predominance of pine also makes the forests one of the last strongholds of a diminishing red squirrel population. Grey squirrels are much more abundant.

The Norfolk Naturalists' Trust reserve at Thompson Water

If you go in May or June you will see broom and gorse in yellow profusion along some of the tracks and rides, and occasionally wild strawberries growing at some of the plantation edges. If you are even luckier you might also catch a glimpse of a grass snake. These are occasionally seen basking in the sun usually near undergrowth. They are generally olive-brown with vertical black bars, are non-poisonous and harmless, and quite happy to see the back of you. The poisonous adder (distinguishable by a dark zigzag along its back) is occasionally found in Norfolk, but it is dangerous only if provoked.

Of the four species of deer found in the forest the largest, red, is usually in small groups on the east side of the afforested area. The next largest, fallow, is concentrated in King's Forest. Roe are also common throughout the plantations and have to be controlled because of the damage they can do, particularly to young trees. The smallest, muntjac, seem to be increasing in numbers. Deer are not easy to spot and are unlikely to be seen in the vicinity of the LDR in summer in any numbers.

The **Stanford Battle Area** is not open to the public, but despite, or perhaps because of, military activity it is a haven for plant and wildlife.

Some 150 years ago much of the land covered by the present training area looked as it does today except for the numerous belts and trees and a lake known as Stanford Water. West of the old Tottington–Thetford road stretched a vast and virtually uninhabited heath—'an ocean of bracken and heather . . . ' observed one writer. Today, fine areas of surviving Breck heathland are preserved behind the fences; and some of the best views, too. Its wide, wooded vistas are unique in Norfolk.

Stone curlew

One of its best known inhabitants is the stone curlew, a shy and rare breeding bird of which there are fewer than 200 pairs in the whole of East Anglia. Its eerie call can sometimes be heard at dusk and during the night. Stone curlew arrive from the Mediterranean in March and depart again in late September or early October.

Despite its timidity it seems to have come to terms with the armed forces, for the birds also nest beside the busy runways of the American fighter-bomber base at RAF Lakenheath. One theory is that although they do not mind noise, they do not particularly trust people. Within the boundaries of the Battle Area, incidentally, the stone curlew often shares its habitat with the wheatear.

More common here than elsewhere in Norfolk are breeding curlew and tree pipits. Among other birds are nightjar, woodlark, English and French partridge, lapwing, flocks of golden plover and many woodland and riverine birds. Over 185 species have been recorded in 20 years.

In 'upland' Norfolk, north of Castle Acre and particularly in the areas around Harpley, Houghton, Bircham and the Massinghams, the ubiquitous rabbit—decimated by myxomatosis in the mid-1950s—holds court, partridge and pheasant haunt the fields, and the verges and hedgerows are often full of hawthorn. This is a good area on a still summer's day to stand awhile and listen to skylarks trilling high above the fields.

Holme-next-the-Sea in some ways represents a dividing line. To the south is inland Norfolk. To the west are the cliffs of Hunstanton and the flatness of the Wash marshes, and to the east the north Norfolk coastline.

The most northerly known termination of the Roman Peddars Way, Holme, boasts two reserves, **Holme Dunes**, managed by the Norfolk Naturalists' Trust, and **Holme Bird Observatory**, to the east of the village, cared for by Norfolk Ornithologists' Association. Here will be found sand-dunes and salt-marsh, each with its own distinct flora including marram grass, sea lavender and samphire, orchids and helleborines. During the autumn birds of all kinds can be observed passing through on their way from the Arctic to more southerly climes.

Black-tailed godwit Spoonbill Oystercatchers
Redshank Ringed plover

Salt-marsh rush　　　Cinnabar moth　Sea lavender　　　Sea aster

The dunes—foreshore and sand-dunes, fresh and salt-water marsh, pine trees and grazing meadows—are rich in insect and plant life, including a variety of orchids. There are many wading birds, among them nesting avocet. According to the time of the year birds which can also be spotted from the hides include bearded tit, water rail, green sandpiper, spotted redshank and greenshank. Elsewhere are snow bunting, shore lark, several warblers, marsh harrier and skuas.

There is a warden at the Bird Observatory, hides and nature trail. So far over 280 species of birds have been recorded.

Titchwell Marsh, the Royal Society for the Protection of Birds' reserve, has an unusual history. Sea walls were built in the 1780s and root crops and beef produced on the enclosed land for nearly 170 years. The tidal surge of January, 1953, destroyed a large part of the northern defences, however, and the area reverted to salt-marsh. Dead trees still in the reed-beds are utilised by marsh harriers. During the Second World War the army also used the area as a tank firing range. The

Scurvy grass

Sea arrowgrass   Glasswort   Sea purslane Sea spurvy Sea wormwood

marsh remained part of a farm estate until 1973 when the
RSPB purchased the freehold of 420 acres, and in 1979 the
immediate foreshore was leased to the society by the Crown
Estate Commissioners.

A variety of habitat, including tidal and freshwater reed-
beds, salt and freshwater marsh, sand-dunes and shingle
beach, is to be found here. There is a visitor centre, too.

Bearded tit, marsh harrier and bittern nest in the reed-
beds; redshank, black-headed gulls and little grebe nest near
the pools, and tern, ringed plover and oystercatchers on the
beach. Many waders visit the pools in spring and autumn
and large flocks of knot can sometimes be seen on the
beach. Winter visitors include Brent geese, goldeneye,
eider, widgeon and sea and hen harriers.

It also embraces a wide range of plant life including sea
sandwort, hornwrack, sea lavender, sea pink, sea aster and
glasswort. It is on the foreshore, too, that the floor of the
ancient forest of oak, alder and elm can often be spotted at
low tide.

Bearded tit

Reed warbler

Bittern

Little grebe

Fen wainscott moth

Water rail

Reed bunting

This is also the home of lugworms, which are dug by professional worm diggers for fishing bait; always providing the curlew and oystercatchers have not eaten them first.

Seal colony

The sand-dunes and marshes of **Blakeney Point**, which is at the end of a continuous ridge of shingle originating beneath the cliffs of Weybourne, $12\frac{1}{2}$ kilometres (8 miles) to the east, has long been a paradise for natural historians. The Point was acquired in 1912 and given to the National Trust, and became one of the first nature reserves established in Norfolk.

It is now managed by a Trust warden who lives during the summer months in the old lifeboat house. The Point can be reached by ferry from Blakeney and Morston quays.

There is a permanent colony of common and grey seals on the sand spits west of the Point, and the numerous habitats which range from shingle bank, sea-shore, sand-dunes and salt-marsh, support a tapestry of plant life. Here can be found sea rocket and sea campion, marsh samphire, sea purslane, thrift and bird's-foot trefoil, and among the dunes, sea bindweed and rosebay willowherb.

It is as a nesting place and migratory channel into England that the Point is best known, and rare species are seen regularly by the many bird watchers who visit Blakeney. In winter the harbour and marshes are the haunt of wildfowl, waders and Brent geese. Among familiar breeding visitors are black-headed gulls, the sandwich, common and little tern, oystercatcher and ring plover.

The National Trust now manages over 16 kilometres (10 miles) of north Norfolk coast, all of which is considered to be of international importance. The most important is Blakeney Point, largely because of the many types of habitat it includes, but **Morston** marshes, **Stiffkey** salt-marshes and **Brancaster** are a unique series of extensive and largely undisturbed salt-marshes. **Salthouse Broad** (including Arnold's Marsh, managed by the Norfolk Naturalists' Trust) is of great interest to ornithologists who come to observe the black-tailed godwit, avocet and rare passage migrants.

Scolt Head Island, which has been a nature reserve since 1923, is also owned by the National Trust and, at the east end, by the Norfolk Naturalists' Trust. In 1953 it was leased to the Nature Conservancy Council and is now managed by a joint committee representing the organisations and local

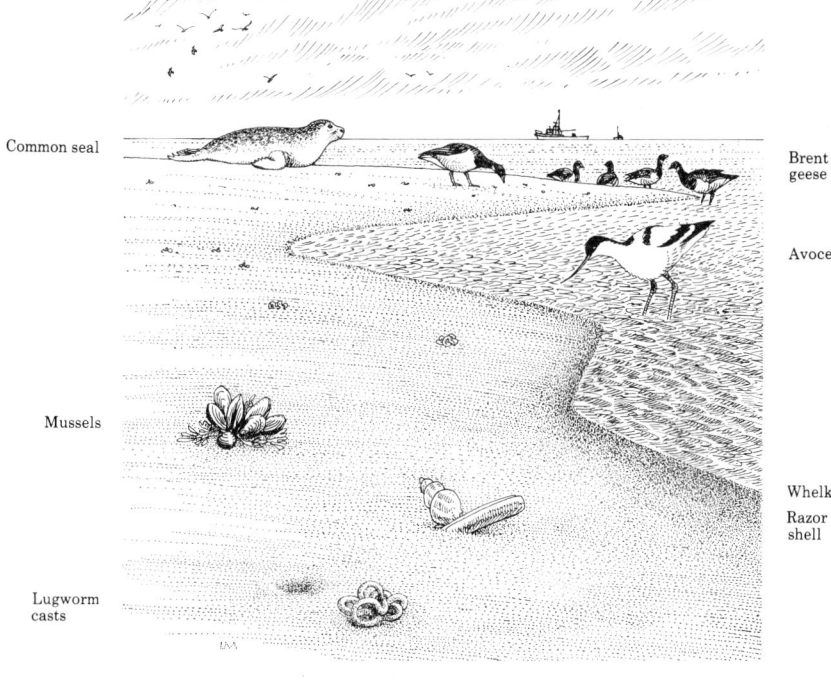

Common seal

Brent geese

Avocet

Mussels

Whelk

Razor shell

Lugworm casts

residents. Access to Scolt, which is a 3½-mile-long shingle ridge, is by boat from Brancaster Staithe.

The 'Meals', which line the coast at **Holkham**, were once sandy islands like Scolt Head. They are now part of the mainland and are covered with Corsican pines. The tide goes out a long way here, leaving lagoons and wide areas of flat sand. A lovely spot, but beware of the returning tide.

Cley marshes, another Norfolk Naturalists' Trust reserve, is visited by permit only (available from the visitor centre). It was established in 1926. The marshes, lagoons and rough grazing are an obvious attraction, and over 270 species of birds have been recorded. There are a number of observation hides, including one for disabled visitors, which give views of breeding avocet, bittern and bearded tit in summer, many species of wildfowl, and visiting rarities such as spoonbill and black-tailed godwit as well as autumn and spring migrants.

This is well known territory to 'twitchers'. In May, 1983, for example, several hundred enthusiasts converged on Cley from all parts of the country to see such rare migrants as spotted, marsh and Terek sandpipers and a red-necked phalarope. A year later 300 'twitchers' turned up to catch a glimpse of a Ross's gull.

Towards the eastern end of the LDR the bluebell woods of **Roman Camp** (which often look their best in May), and occasional patches of brilliant red poppies in the Cromer area in summer, provide a different and yet appealing final phase of the walk.

History of the Peddars Way

Tales of the romance of the open road always seem a bit thin to me. Authors rarely take into account the limitations and inconveniences of unmaintained or unmetalled routes. Frankly, I cannot conceive of a more uncomfortable mode of transport than coaching in winter despite the rosy glow of traditional Christmas card scenes.

Even so, the 'romance' has kept interest alive. In Norfolk, 15 years ago, few people actually strolled along the Peddars Way. Now hundreds do so.

Some of the old tales still cling, particularly to the Peddars Way and to its near neighbour the Icknield Way.

One tale suggests that the line of the Peddars Way is much older than the Roman period—and that it may have been the 'war road' of the Iceni. There is no evidence to support either theory.

The best historical judgement at present is that the road which subsequently became known as the Peddars Way was built by the Romans in the years immediately after AD 61. It was born of a political and military necessity forged in the aftermath of war. Today's broader view enables us to add that it is now one of the most important, substantial and best-preserved Roman roads in Norfolk.

To trace its roots it is useful to go back further than the Boudican revolt of AD 61, for the road's line from the Suffolk border to the north-west Norfolk coast is also linked to the great chalk ridge and thus by proximity to the Norfolk length of the Icknield Way. That in turn takes us back before the coming of the Romans.

It seems at least possible that the Icknield Way had its origins in animal migration routes perhaps about 8,000 BC (radio-carbon dating). Very little is known about it. What is clear is that there was a line of communication along the upper and lower reaches of the chalk ridge and that it seems to have provided an important route for many hundreds of years. It was certainly used as a trade route during the Neolithic period.

In terms of the Icknield's pre-Roman appearance, the concept of a single continuous track must be discarded.

Village names —
ancient and
modern

Obstructions, diversions, weather conditions, watercourses and changing terrain would have brought alternative tracks into use at an early stage. It is more likely to have comprised a wide swathe of routes meandering in roughly the same direction.

Incidentally, one recent suggestion is that the Ordnance Survey marked Icknield Way in the north-west of the county may, in fact, be the medieval line, in which case the older pre-Roman tracks would have been even further to the west and closer to the sea.

Emergence of the Bronze Age heralded substantial technical progress. Nearly 600 findspots of Bronze Age metal-work have been recorded in the county.

The appearance of weapons and gear such as harness and wagon fittings is indicative of a stratified warrior society. By about 1,000 BC communities often lived in small groups of thatched round houses surrounded by palisades set among well-ordered fields, either ploughed or given over to grazing.

The Iceni

The groups which collectively became known as the Iceni may have belonged originally to Belgium and Holland, having crossed the North Sea and made landfall on the Wash or along the rivers Waveney and Yare. Later, bands of aristocratic warriors arrived from the Marne valley.

What became known as the **Snettisham** treasure, which included a remarkable gold torc, and another hoard from **Sedgeford**, found in 1965, seem to relate to this period. Many of the objects were connected with horses and chariots—not the type of chariot represented in the Victorian statue group by London's Westminster Bridge, but a lighter bladeless vehicle more suitable for displays of bravado than for actual fighting.

Earthworks at Narborough, Warham, Holkham and South Creake fit somewhere into an elaborate background, as does a recently excavated, enigmatic, and unusual timber construction at **Gallows Hill**, Thetford. Clearly, it was a place of some importance, though there is a reluctance at the moment to describe it either as royal or as a palace.

Some of these sites may, of course, have been defensive constructions against other tribes, such as the Catuvellauni.

Iceni coinage began to appear about 10 BC (including boar-horse, face-horse, and pattern-horse varieties) and continued to the time of the Boudican rebellion. Coin-scatters from 11 Iceni coin hoards further suggest there might have been at least three tribes, or tribal centres, perhaps in some sort of loose federation, based in north-west Norfolk, in the vicinity of Norwich, and in Breckland. The theory is given added support by suggestions of early Roman forts, marching camps or policing posts at Threxton and Horstead.

Gold tubular torcs from the Snettisham treasure *c.* 25 BC

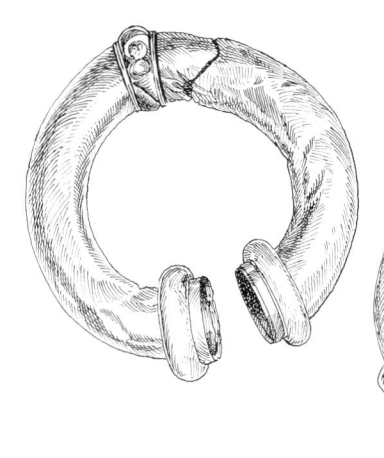

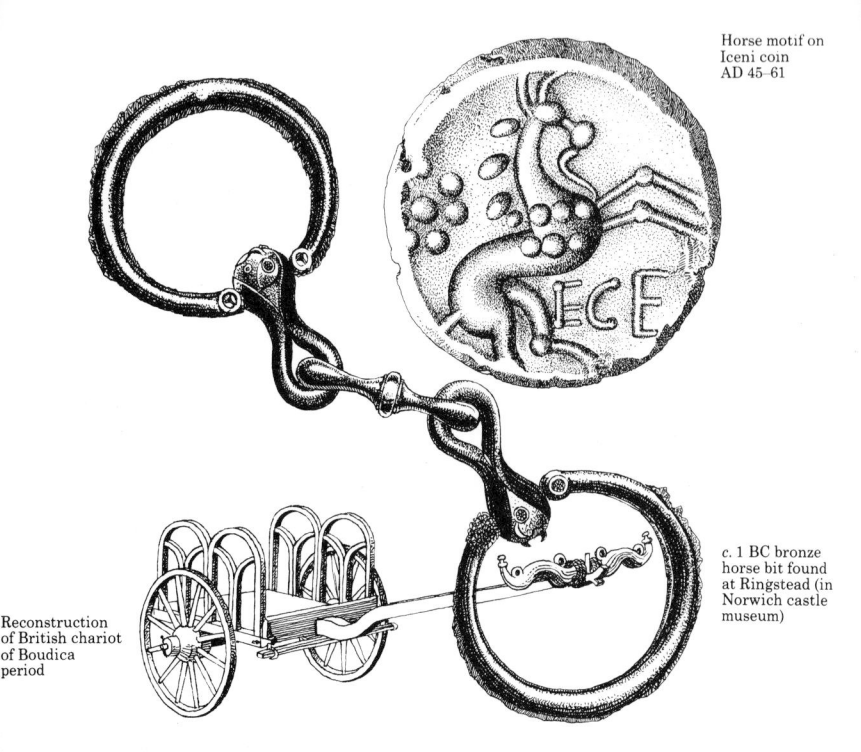

Horse motif on
Iceni coin
AD 45–61

c. 1 BC bronze
horse bit found
at Ringstead (in
Norwich castle
museum)

Reconstruction
of British chariot
of Boudica
period

The Iceni are thought to have been initially friendly towards the Roman invaders. At least, the tribe is included on Caesar's list of peoples who sought alliance with Rome. They and others may for a time have formed a bloc of pro-Roman tribes.

The years that followed brought a period of increasing unrest leading to a quickly crushed uprising in AD 47, then a continuing growth of bitter feeling which culminated in the bloody revolt of AD 61.

The revolt

Surprisingly little is known of **Boudica**, save comments by one Roman writer that she was 'huge of frame, terrifying of aspect, and with a harsh voice. A great mass of bright red hair fell to her knees; she wore a great twisted golden neck-lace, and a tunic of many colours . . .' The vividness of the description disguises the fact that—except for the events of a few short weeks in her life—nothing is known of her. No records exist that state where she came from, who she was, how old she was; or what was the driving force which enabled her to mobilise many of the tribes and, in a final battle, field a wild and undisciplined army numbering perhaps 100,000.

She must have been a woman of considerable personal charisma.

The events of the revolt are known to most school children. The horde fell upon Colchester and then on London and St. Albans.

Thousands were killed. Boudica, it is thought took poison, although that is not certain. The outcome, however, was inevitable. The Iceni tribal system was destroyed and dispersed, never again to rise, and the way left open for more than 300 years of Roman rule.

The fact that the Peddars Way is a Roman road of military proportion suggests it was constructed during the 'policing' period immediately following the Boudican revolt. It may even have been built to link a string of Roman forts. By implication, therefore, it may also have been one of the first, if not the first, Roman road in the area, for it seems clear it was related in the initial stages to the subjugation of the Iceni tribal heartland and the need to provide a suitable surface for the fast transportation of men and materials. Nothing is known of its seaward terminus, but there may have been anchorage near Holme or perhaps a ferry service across the Wash.

The Peddars Way could once have been linked directly with Colchester.

In some places it was built on a substantial **agger**, or embankment, of local materials. Parts of it were 13 metres (45 feet) wide. At Brettenham it was a causeway 4½ metres (16 feet) wide at base, 76 centimetres (2 feet 6 inches) thick in the centre, and made of rammed flint topped with gravel. On the

The Norman castle at Castle Acre

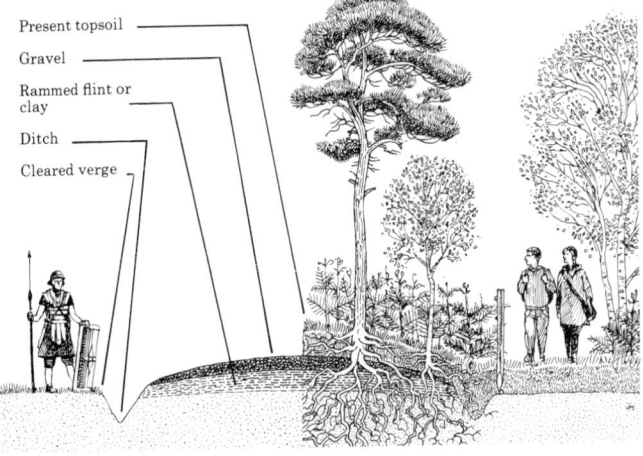

Present topsoil
Gravel
Rammed flint or clay
Ditch
Cleared verge

The Roman road near Brettenham, then and now

east side the rammed flint continued as a path, or lay-by, at least 1¼ metres (4 feet) wide. Another nearby section of the agger was built of a rammed chalky boulder clay, with a ditch on either side.

Road network

In Norfolk the length of known Roman and Romanised roads and tracks, including the Icknield Way, amounts to about 386 kilometres (240 miles), while a further 128 kilometres (80 miles), at least, seem possible. The actual figure was almost certainly much higher.

Only one, the Peddars Way, seems to have been of military proportion. The others ranged from roads to lanes and tracks to paths. Even so, the Peddars Way is unlikely to have been a replacement for the Icknield Way. These two lines of communication sprang from different sources; and the Peddars Way which, in general, hugs the higher ground, was clearly made for fast transport and not for farm carts. It is also possible that a military requirement for the road faded at an early date, for relative peace and comparative prosperity seem to have been established fairly quickly.

The Romanised Icknield Way linked numerous farming enterprises and there were villas, for example, at Grimston and Gayton Thorpe. Roads seem to have linked the two routes.

Communities also sprang up beside the Peddars Way. At Brettenham large quantities of Roman material have been found; and although nothing now remains above ground a site in the parish of Saham Toney may once have been the principal market town in western Iceni territory.

The Early Saxons, with their lack of wealth and small self-contained communities, had no need of highways of Roman size and directness. Consequently, some communities, including a few in the north-west of the county, seem to stand aside from the Peddars Way.

The Roman roads decayed over the centuries, and the Way began to fragment.

Sections of it were undoubtedly utilised by medieval pilgrims heading for Walsingham and it had also been used for the movement of stock, for other agricultural purposes, and for over half its length as a parish boundary marker. A few lengths disappeared altogether many years ago.

Why is the Way called Peddars?

Well, there are several points to bear in mind. First, the *name* is certainly not Roman. It is more probably a 15th- or 16th-century attachment which has survived only here. For example, a stretch of the Icknield Way was referred to as 'Peddersty alias Saltersty' during the reign of Henry IV, and a path leading to Lessingham church was marked on a map of 1587 as 'Peddars Weye'. In 1845 the Roman road was referred to as 'Pedlars Way'. Peddars Way may therefore be little more than a generic name for a footpath.

In the 18th century a ped was a semi-circular basket for carrying produce, and Norwich once had a 'ped market' where women sat in rows on the cobbles selling produce. Perhaps the Peddars Way was used to transport local produce, too.

If so, it is nice to think that even today some sections of this old road still help to service local farms and fields.

Knettishall to Merton

19 kilometres (11½ miles)

These first few kilometres provide some easy walking along one of the nicest stretches of the Peddars Way. There are two narrow rivers to cross as the landscape slowly evolves from wooded river valley to forestry plantation, and from heath to modern arable farmland. In spring and summer, particularly, Breckland has a special character of its own—forest fringed fields, belts of gnarled Scots pines, dark plantations, heat and flint and dust, heaths and paths and, some say, a rather special sort of light. Close to Merton the walker may encounter the inhabitants of another Breckland habitat: soldiers, in the Stanford Battle Area.

Knettishall Country Park provides a lovely backcloth to the start of the LDR. The heath dips gently towards woodlands which rim the horizon and briefly hide the Little Ouse river from view. The river is the boundary between Suffolk and Norfolk, so the route's actual flirtation with Suffolk is brief, lasting no more than a few minutes' stroll.

Begin on the Peddars Way at the acorn waymark and information board opposite Blackwater Carr beside the road at the western edge of the park.

Ignore waymarks displaying a white arrow on a green background. These relate to circular walks round the park. Simply cross the road and follow a clearly discernible route into the trees. Walk the woodland footpath for almost 700 metres then bear right and cross the footbridge over the river.

This crossing place is known as Blackwater, a not uncommon name in East Anglia. A map of 1797 shows that a number of roads and paths once converged here, as parish boundaries still do. Standing on the river bank it is easy to see that the route of the Peddars Way, to the rear and (roughly indicated by the line of trees) on the far side, is not in precise alignment. One reason is that the Roman engineers seem to have incorporated a Z-bend, a fairly common device, to enable the road to approach the ford. Also, over the centuries and because of changing conditions, the most favourable crossing places would not necessarily have remained in exactly the same location.

Disused railway
near Stonebridge

A couple of kilometres to the east at this point is Riddlesworth, a girls' private boarding school. One of its most famous former pupils is Diana, Princess of Wales.

Once over the bridge continue for about 200 metres and then turn left and follow the path along a thick belt of trees. The agger (embankment) can be seen again once the Thetford–Diss and Thetford–East Harling roads have been crossed in quick succession, the linking section being a short length of redundant metalled road now used as a highways' maintenance dump. To the west, between screens of trees, is Shadwell Park, a substantial agricultural estate.

The crossing of the Thetford–Diss road marks the beginning of the Forestry Commission plantation, and at Thorpe Woodlands (or Thorpe Farm), which is a Commission camping and caravan site (alas, unsuitable for backpackers), the Peddars Way provides a sort of buffer or boundary between the two woodlands.

The Roman road as it approaches the river Thet is again raised on an embankment (the bank helped to give rise to the expression 'high road', meaning a road of importance) but on this stretch the agger is fenced and private. The path follows the eastern edge of the agger, which is overgrown in places and marked by a line of trees and bushes, and then makes off across the river meadow and turns right for a short distance along the river bank to a footbridge at a place called Droveway Ford. After rain the path across the meadow can be wet and muddy, and along by the river it is very narrow in places. Take care not to slip.

Once again the lines of the Peddars Way on either side of the river are not in alignment, and it is difficult to decide where the original ford might have been. The river has been dredged and altered and there is no certain evidence of a paved ford, or for that matter of any sort of Roman bridge.

Deserted settlements

This is a fascinating area. There are Anglo-Saxon and Romano-British sites in nearby Brettenham (which may mean 'the Briton' or 'Britons' according to Eilert Ekwall's *Dictionary of English Place-Names*), and an important Iron Age riverside site at Micklemoor Hill about 3 kilometres to the east. West Harling, Middle Harling and Harling Thorpe, now known as **Thorpe Woodlands**, are all deserted settlement sites which were in separate and thriving existence throughout most of the medieval period. The West Harling settlement embraced several streets. Other streets, including Thorpe, seem to have been detached. All three had largely disappeared by about 1735.

Nowadays this is a peaceful spot and the plantations, which incorporate footpaths as well as discreet sites for tents and caravans, are enjoyed by hundreds of visitors each year. The unruffled river is a casual and calming influence. The forests, of course, invoke their own form of stillness and serenity.

Once over the river Thet, and having crossed the Brettenham road, the path continues along a belt of trees and then follows the edges of pine plantations for about 2 kilometres to the A11, the main Norwich–London trunk road.

The path crosses undulating countryside most of the way from the river, and on windless days in summer it can be very hot here. To the west the remains of Brettenham heath, dotted with hawthorn bushes, provides an inkling of what some of the open areas used to be like. This national nature reserve, leased, fenced and protected by the Nature Conservancy Council, is one of the largest slices of remaining Breckland heath. The views towards Thetford are expansive and invigorating, and there is the smell of pine all along this section.

The most disturbing noise, other than the murmur of distant traffic, is likely to be provided by passing jet aircraft. A rule-of-thumb guide here and for elsewhere in Norfolk is that the American F-111s and A-10s may originate from bases at Lakenheath and Bentwaters, respectively, while the British contribution tends to be dominated by Jaguars from Coltishall and Tornados from Marham and Honington. On particularly noisy days Mildenhall will lend a hand, too, usually with large American transport aircraft.

Once over the stile to the south of the A11, and having crossed a minor road, the Peddars Way slowly loses some of its serenity to become little more than a pot-holed track. Extreme care is required when crossing the busy A11, for the traffic travels quickly. Equal care must be taken passing over the railway level-crossing.

Immediately over the crossing, and just beyond the railway house, the track coming in from the west to join the Peddars Way is the Harling Drove, or Great Fen Road, of unknown age and origin but certainly pre-Roman. Later, it was improved and used by the Romans and later still, and before the coming of the railways, it was a busy route for drovers with flocks of sheep and herds of cattle. Its western end seems to have been near Hockwold on the edge of the Fens. Nearer to the Peddars Way it keeps noticeably close to a number of Breckland meres and watering places including Lang Mere and Ring Mere.

Ring Mere, particularly, attracts paths and parish boundaries as pollen attracts bees, and there is a possibility this may have been Hringmara, site of the battle of AD 1010 between the Danes and the Saxons under Ulfcytel. In the end the home side was slaughtered, leaving the Danes free to harry the countryside for three months and sack Thetford for the umpteenth time.

Part of a translation of a Danish saga reads:

> 'From Hringmara field
> The chime of war,
> Sword striking shield
> Rings from afar;
> The living fly,
> The dead piled high
> The moor enrich;
> Red runs the ditch'.

Another saga proclaims that 'Hringmara Heath was a bed of death' and explains how 'Haarfager's heir dealt slaughter there'.

A short distance beyond the Harling Drove is a natural gas pipeline service station (the pipe travels from the Bacton coastal terminal to the Midlands). Then on the opposite side there are faint signs of the old Thetford–Watton railway line. The outline and surface of the path soften as grass begins to intrude again, and there is one nice green and hedged section bordered by a line of ancient pines. Then the path passes between the abutments of an abandoned railway bridge, bears briefly left then right, and emerges on the Hockham road at East Wretham (or Stonebridge).

The Dog & Partridge public house, which has played host to neighbouring soldiery for many years is now becoming familiar to increasing numbers of walkers. Just beyond the pub the path turns left and leaves the main road. The former Wretham Park estate, with its ruined church, is hidden among the trees to the west, while the first plantation on the same side is Brickkiln Covert.

Even though the road is metalled here this is still the ancient line of the Peddars Way, though it is always possible its course has been amended in places. At Galley Hill, which is about 46 metres (150 feet) above sea-level, and a parish boundary, the gentle curve of the Peddars Way marks the only major shift in direction along the entire length of the Roman road. The road is metalled because, among other reasons, it is used by military vehicles. Between Galley Hill and Cranberry Rough, however, the military road swings left (this is the old road to Tottington) to enter the prohibited Battle Area, while the Peddars Way, which continues straight on, reverts to a rough stony surface.

Military activity

A few words about the **Battle Area**.

The walker may or may not see evidence of military activity, but he may be certain the Army is there in strength. On quiet days and weekends there may be little to see other than the passage of military vehicles. If a major exercise is in progress, however, more evidence may be apparent. There

Military area north of Thompson

could be aerial activity (Hercules transports, helicopters, and sometimes parachutists), increased road activity, and lots of muffled bumps and bangs. By night there may also be the flashes and bumps of aerial reconnaissance 'photo-flash' activity.

It is not unknown for passers-by to become unwittingly involved. The line of the Way, particularly between Flag Heath and the Merton estate, actually runs through a section of the Battle Area, and just occasionally the simulated 'fighting' spills over on to both sides of the track. Black-faced camouflaged infantrymen occasionally lurk in the bracken and they have been known, during exercises and when guarding against 'intruders', to stop passers-by and ask for some form of identification. This has happened to me on the public path, but it is very rare. On one occasion, though, I did have to stop and wait while infantrymen 'fought' a noisy 'battle' among the undergrowth 100 metres further along the Way.

Much of the land hereabouts was enclosed in about 1817 and Flag Heath, for example, may refer to turf cutting. In 1845 a tributary of the river Wissey was dammed and allowed to flood, creating what is now known as **Thompson Water**. The walker catches a first glimpse of this beautiful and secluded lake not far from the site of the old ford. The Water and Thompson Common (see Wildlife and nature reserves) constitute a relatively new reserve to which the public have free access and there is satisfaction in the notion that both are now protected.

The walker may pause at this point and, military activities permitting, enjoy the peace and the feeling of isolation. Thompson Water and Willie's Clump, alongside the Peddars Way, is a lovely spot despite the proximity of the sinister sounding Madhouse Plantation. Willie's Clump, with its memorial plaque, comprises about 170 trees and shrubs including oak, rowan, birch, field maple, hazel, hawthorn and guelder rose.

Anyone wishing to visit Thompson village, and its thatched pub, has a pleasant 20-minute walk ahead after turning right just beyond Thompson Water.

After crossing the road beyond Thompson Water there are further occasional glimpses between the trees of the original character of some of the Breckland heaths, and then the curiously named Shakers Furze plantation. There have been a number of attempts to explain the name, for Shakers is also applied to a few other places and roads in the area (just as 'Smugglers' is applied to a road presently in the Battle Area,

Cottages at Merton

and which may have been part of the Icknield Way). The name would appear to have no connection with the Shakers' sect or, as some have suggested, with shaking (ie, blowing) sands. One school of thought suggests it recalls shimmering aspen (Populus tremula) trees.

Over Sparrow Hill the route skirts the edges of **Merton** estate, one of the great estates of Norfolk. The present owner, Lord Walsingham, facilitated the opening of this stretch of the path and indeed assisted with its physical establishment.

Merton is thought to mean 'the town by the mere', and there are Roman associations with the area. In the estate, as the walker will see, are many fine old trees. Not far from Merton on the Watton–Great Hockham road is Wayland Wood where the story of *Babes in the Wood* is said to have unfolded. It stands in the ancient Hundred of Wayland. Edward FitzGerald, translator of the *Rubáiyát of Omar Khayyám,* died in Merton while staying with the rector, George Crabbe.

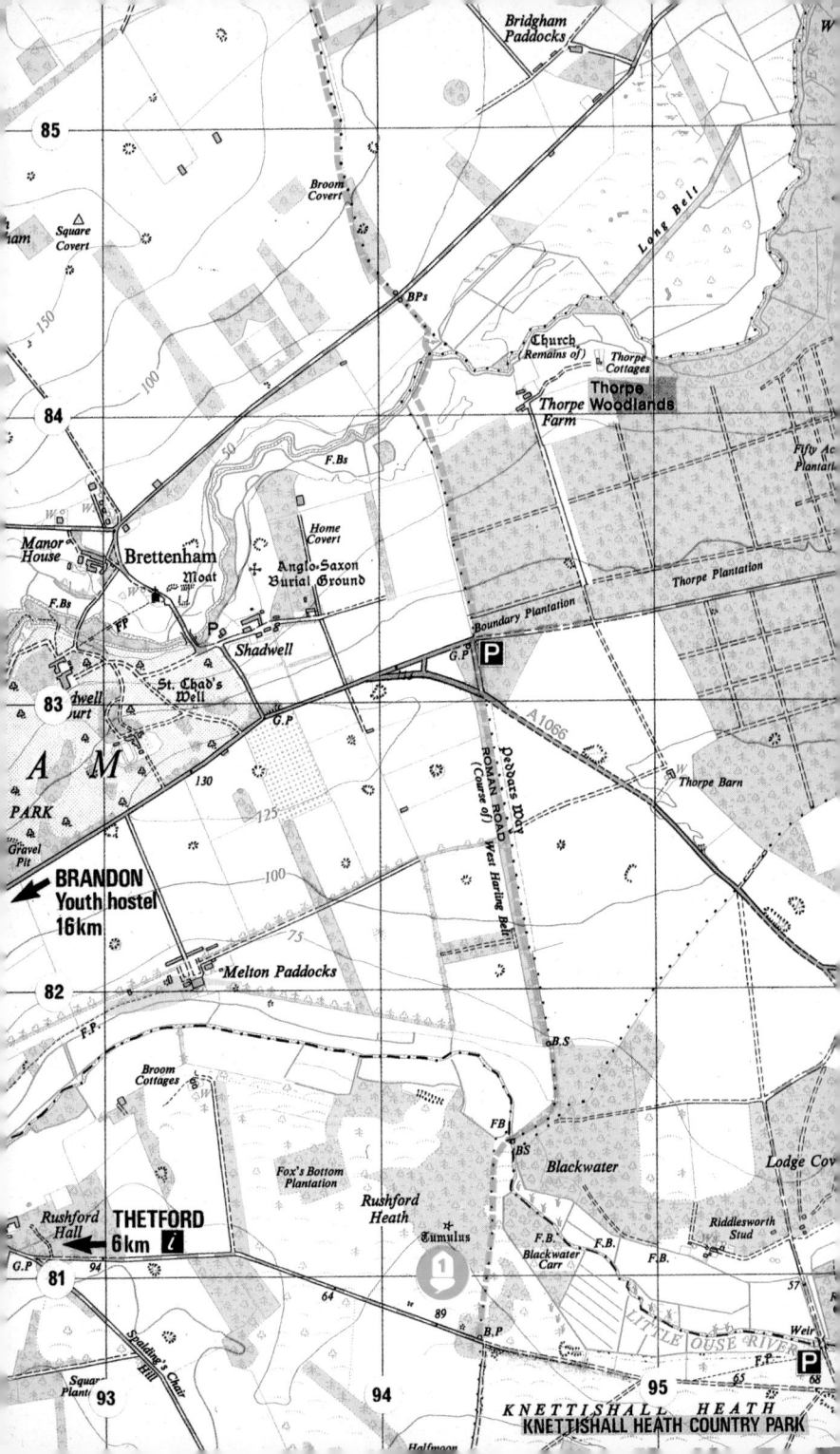

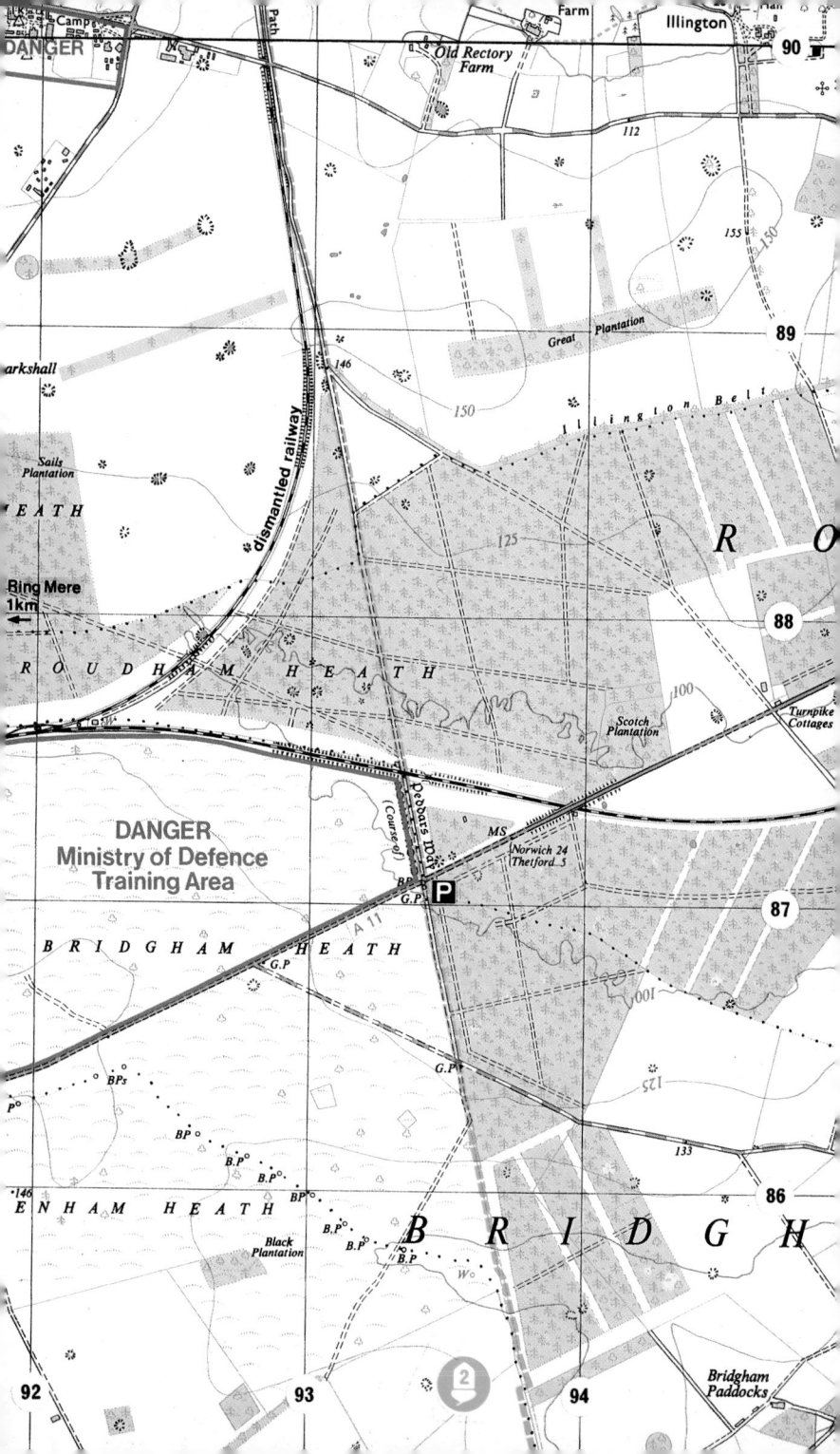

Merton to Castle Acre

23 kilometres (14½ miles)

Much of the ancient line of the Peddars Way from Threxton to North Pickenham, and between Palgrave and Castle Acre, was lost many years ago. This section of the LDR is thus fragmented in a sense that, although it follows the old road as closely as possible, it also incorporates a number of modern alternatives including newly designated footpaths and quiet country lanes. A good slice of it is on metalled surfaces. Even so, the walking is relatively easy and the route loses none of its rural aspect or interest.

A clearly defined path follows the western edge of the **Merton** estate and picks up a metalled road by Home Farm. At the crossroads it turns left on to a bridleway. Some 750 metres further on the track swings right and eventually joins the B1108 Bodney–Watton road. Turn left here but stay on the same side, making careful use of the verge and path until Threxton Crossways is reached.

The market town of Watton is to the east, about 2½ kilometres away, while the round tower church of Threxton can be glimpsed to the north. The church, of Saxon origin, was enlarged in the 13th century.

Not far from here (though there is nothing to be seen of it) is the site of a once substantial Romano-British settlement. Beyond Little Cressingham is an important group of tumuli one of which, when excavated many years ago, produced a rich and elaborate Wessex culture internment. Another Little Cressingham round barrow, excavated more recently and given radio-carbon dating of about 1600 BC, gave no indication of a grave. Studies showed the site was open grassland when the barrow was built; the primeval forest had gone, and there was evidence of arable land use in the vicinity.

At Threxton Crossways cross over the main road with care, continue in the same direction, and then follow the signpost into **Little Cressingham** village. Turn right opposite the White Horse pub. There is now a straightforward walk to the Houghton Springs area.

Shortly after leaving Little Cressingham the route crosses a tributary of the river Wissey. It continues over Caudle Common towards South Pickenham as a narrow and generally quiet country lane which ribbons over an undulating, fertile and nicely wooded landscape.

Just short of the South Pickenham–Ashill crossroads, opposite Hall Farm, the route moves on to a footpath. Pass over the crossroads and continue on the roadside verge and the track on the west side of the hedge. The path runs parallel with the lane past Houghton Carr and over tracks leading left and right to Houghton Springs and Houghton Farm. Then suddenly it swings left beside a hedge and, following the field headlands, zigzags right and left down to the footbridge over the river Wissey, which is quite narrow at this point.

Before turning left and beginning the descent to the river valley a glance behind may reveal the distant and indistinct ruins of the former church of St. Mary, Houghton-on-the-Hill, covered by ivy and surrounded by a thicket. Ahead, the village of **North Pickenham** can be seen on the far side of the river, while beyond the village a large tower makes a useful marker. This is a 170-metre (350-feet) post office microwave relay tower, not far from the former North Pickenham airbase.

Now we are deep in pilgrim country, and many hundreds of travellers making their way to and from Walsingham surely passed through this green valley. The sites of a number of chapels dot the district, including a chapel, hermitage and holy well dedicated to St. Paul, just outside North Pickenham. The Rev. L. E. Whatmore, in his book *Highway to Walsingham* (Pilgrim Bureau, 1973) associates this vicinity with the 'Picnamwade' of Henry VI's journey to Walsingham in 1447. He also records that Charles Brandon, Duke of Suffolk, in a letter to Henry VIII dated 1517, said he met Queen Catherine of Aragon at 'Pykenham Wade' and accompanied her the rest of the way to Walsingham.

Once over the bridge turn right and follow the river towards the village. The path incorporates another zigzag before it joins the South Pickenham road. Turn right and then left at the T-junction and follow the road as far as the Swaffham road. Cross over and rejoin the original line of the Peddars Way as it reverts once more to a grassy track and passes between the abutments of a disused railway bridge.

Curious history

The relay tower now seems quite close, and the old airfield is only a short distance away. The base has a curious history. It was built for the Americans during the Second World War and became the home, briefly, of the 'hard luck' 492nd Bomb

Old mill nea Little Cressingha

54

Bridge over
River Wissey at
South
Pickenham

Group equipped with B-24 Liberators. The Group was operational a mere three months because, between May and August, 1944, it flew 64 missions and lost over 50 aircraft. In 1945 the USAAF evacuated the base, which passed to the RAF. A great deal of construction work was undertaken in the 1950s including the building of three launch pads. In 1959 the presence of 60 Thor ballistic missiles sparked a huge CND demonstration. The missile site was dismantled in 1963 and the airfield then used as a test area for Hawker Siddeley's P1127 Kestrel, forerunner of the Harrier.

Remnants of the railway bridge act as a memorial to the old Swaffham–Thetford railway, which opened in 1875 and closed in 1964. There is a certain irony here. The Roman road lost its general usefulness many years ago and for a long time was totally dominated at this point by the railway line and bridge. Now the railway has departed, the bridge is partially dismantled and some of the embankment bulldozed flat. The Peddars Way, on the other hand, is becoming increasingly busy again.

The bridge also acts as a gateway or entrance to a generally wide and very nice 2½-kilometre stretch of the route known as **Procession Way**. Its name is thought to echo the ceremony of the beating of bounds, for a number of parish boundaries congregate hereabouts. Procession Way is also the meeting place of a number of tracks including, after about 1½ kilometres, a set of crossroads beside Dalton's Plantation which also marks the route's junction with the Swaefas Way (see Additional walks), after the Swabian (Upper Rhine) immigrants who gave Swaffham its name. From here it is possible to divert into the town.

Dalton's plantation near Petygards

The LDR moves on between hedges and trees towards the murmur of distant traffic on the main A47 road. In general it keeps a fairly low profile, which means it is sometimes wet and muddy. To the east Petygards is a landholding which takes it name from the Petigard family; and nearby is the site of a deserted village known as Cotes. One of its boundaries seems to have coincided with the line of another Roman road which once branched from the Peddars Way at North Pickenham towards Toftrees and which, in the 16th century, was known as Walsingham Way and used by pilgrims. Cotes village evidently survived into the 17th century, and Cotes common was enclosed about 1806.

There is an abrupt return to the 20th century when the path suddenly emerges at the side of the A47. The main road is always busy and the traffic fast-moving. Once upon a time there was a tollgate near there.

Cross the road and pass on to the metalled surface of the Peddars Way which now runs for about $1\frac{1}{2}$ kilometres before it swings left to cross the old Swaffham–East Dereham railway line, and then right and left towards **Palgrave Hall**.

Between Palgrave and a distant farm which sits astride a T-junction is a metalled road used mainly as a farm road. Beyond the T-junction, where a moat is marked on the map, are the sites of two more deserted medieval villages, Great and Little Palgrave.

Priory ruins near Castle Acre

Over the hills

At the junction the original line of the Peddars Way is lost once more, though it may have continued over Hungry Hill towards Castle Acre. Instead, the LDR turns left and descends along a minor road to the junction at Bartholomew's Hills.

Six or seven roads and tracks converge here, and it was clearly a crossroads of importance. One of the converging roads, which continues as the main road towards Fakenham, was the west–east Denver–Smallburgh Roman road. This was the eastern end of the Fen Causeway which began near Peterborough. To the south-west of Castle Acre it is known as the Fincham Drove.

Cross the A1045 and follow the road signposted to South Acre which, after a short climb, bears right and rises toward another crossroads. Castle Acre priory and church can now be seen in the distance. Go along the path marked 'Ford', cross the river Nar by the little bridge, and turn right and then left to enter **Castle Acre** by climbing the hill by the Old Red Lion hostel, on the right, and passing under the Bailey Gate leading to Stocks Green.

This is a tranquil area. The small hamlet of South Acre is to the west and there are fine views, in the vicinity of the old ford, of the ruins of the Cluniac priory.

Castle Acre is delightful and well worth a short stay, for it is enhanced by its ruins and earthworks. It is dispersed around a small green, framed by the Bailey Gate, and graced by some fine pubs. Its commanding aspect above a crossing-point of the Nar, and its position astride the Peddars Way, suggests early origins, but surprisingly little evidence of Roman activity has come to light so far. Whether there was an early Roman military or Romano-British settlement here is a matter for speculation.

The village takes its name from its important Norman castle, built during the 11th century, and now huddles around an outer bailey of which only the Bailey Gate survives. Its two round towers date from the 13th century. The south gate was demolished in the last century. Between the castle and the priory is the church of St. James.

The priory itself sits by the north bank of the river. Founded by William de Warenne as a daughter house of the Priory of St. Pancras, Lewes, it later became independent. It was sorely affected by the Dissolution of 1537, and there was some quarrying of the stonework; but the ruins and grounds are impressive and truly delightful.

Indeed, during the summer months the attractions of Castle Acre lure an influx of visitors who come to stroll and relax. It is a nice place in which to do both. Castle Acre is a tidy, quiet, compact hillside village enhanced by impressive ruins and flinty houses and cottages.

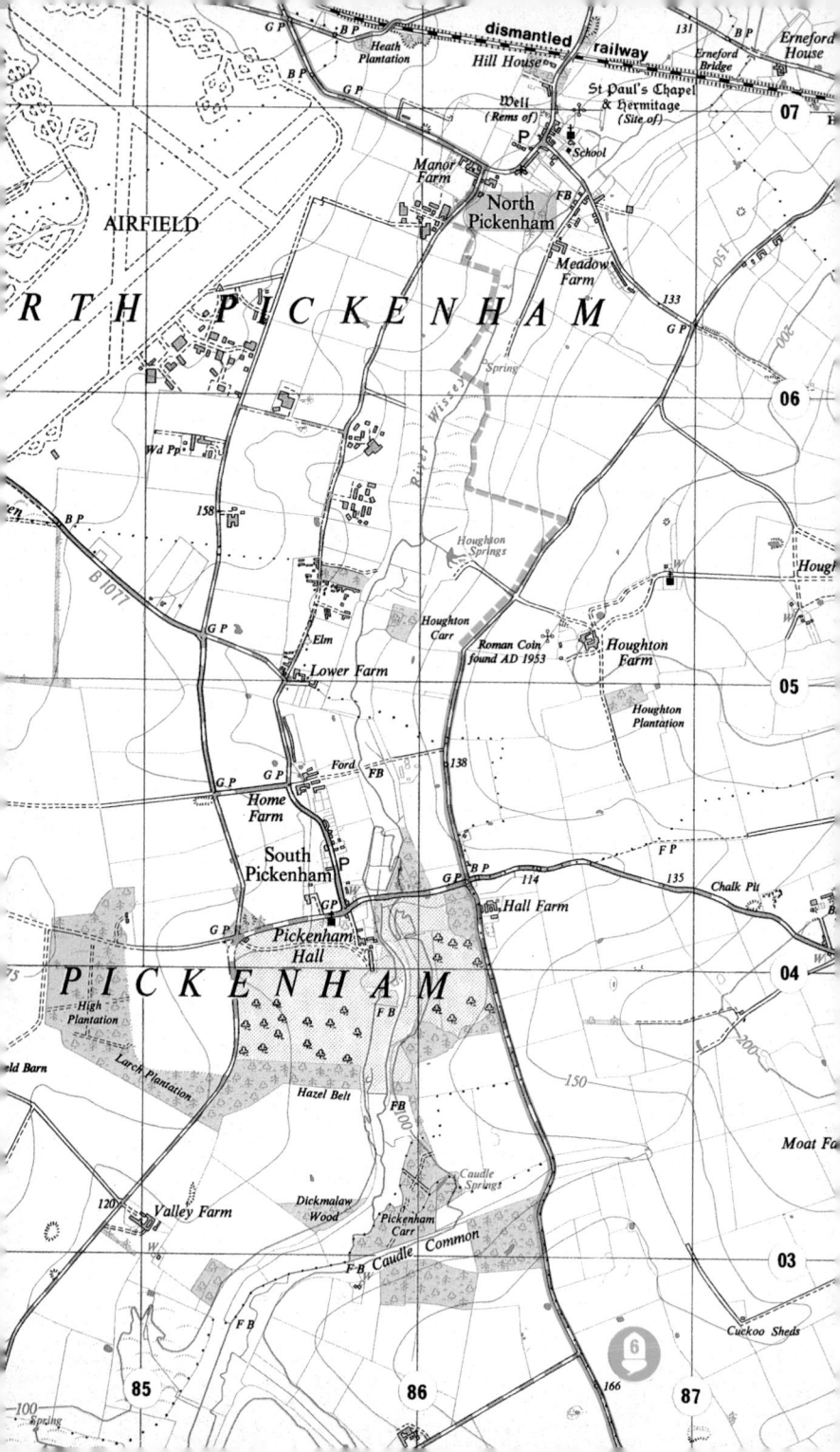

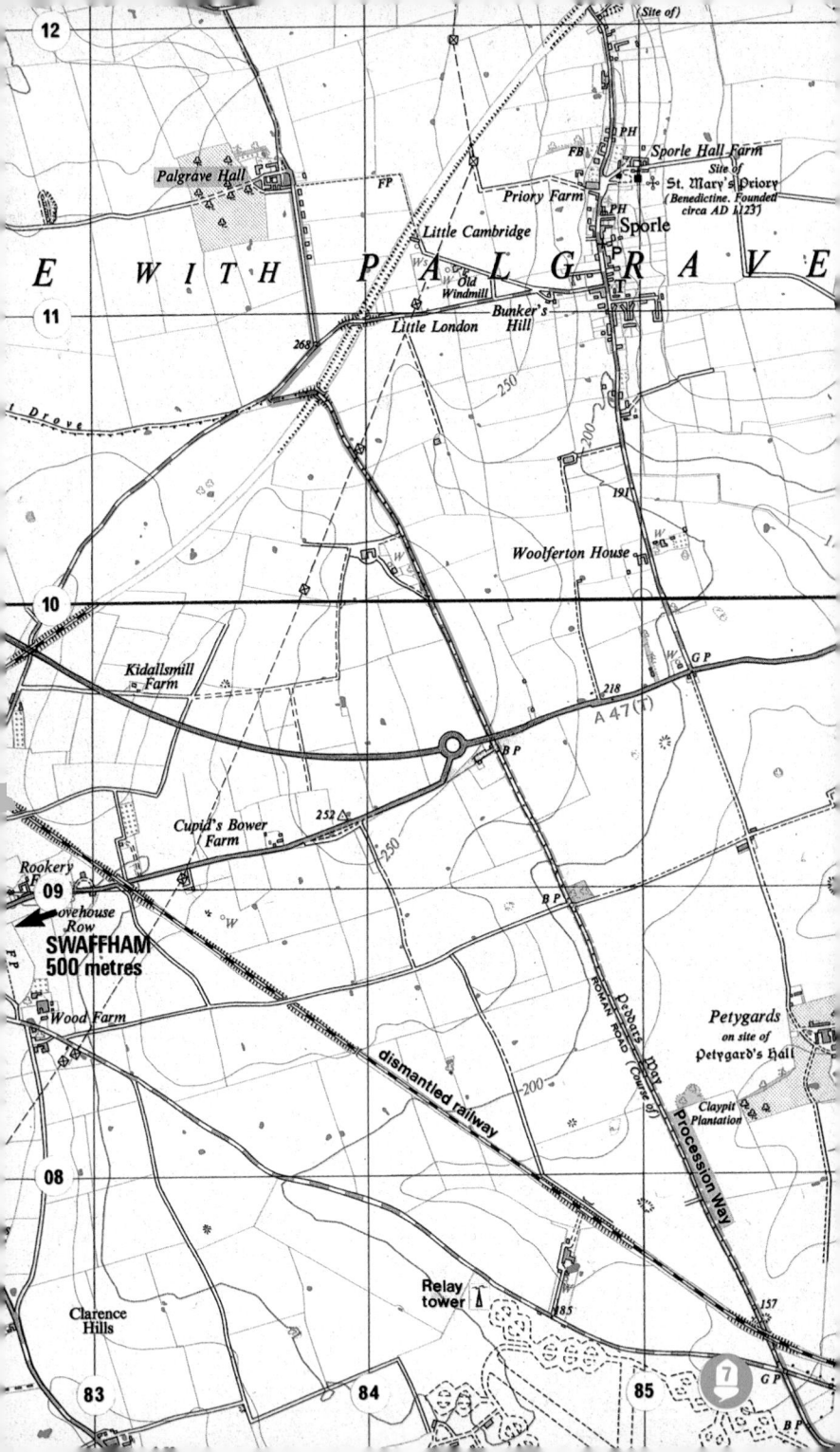

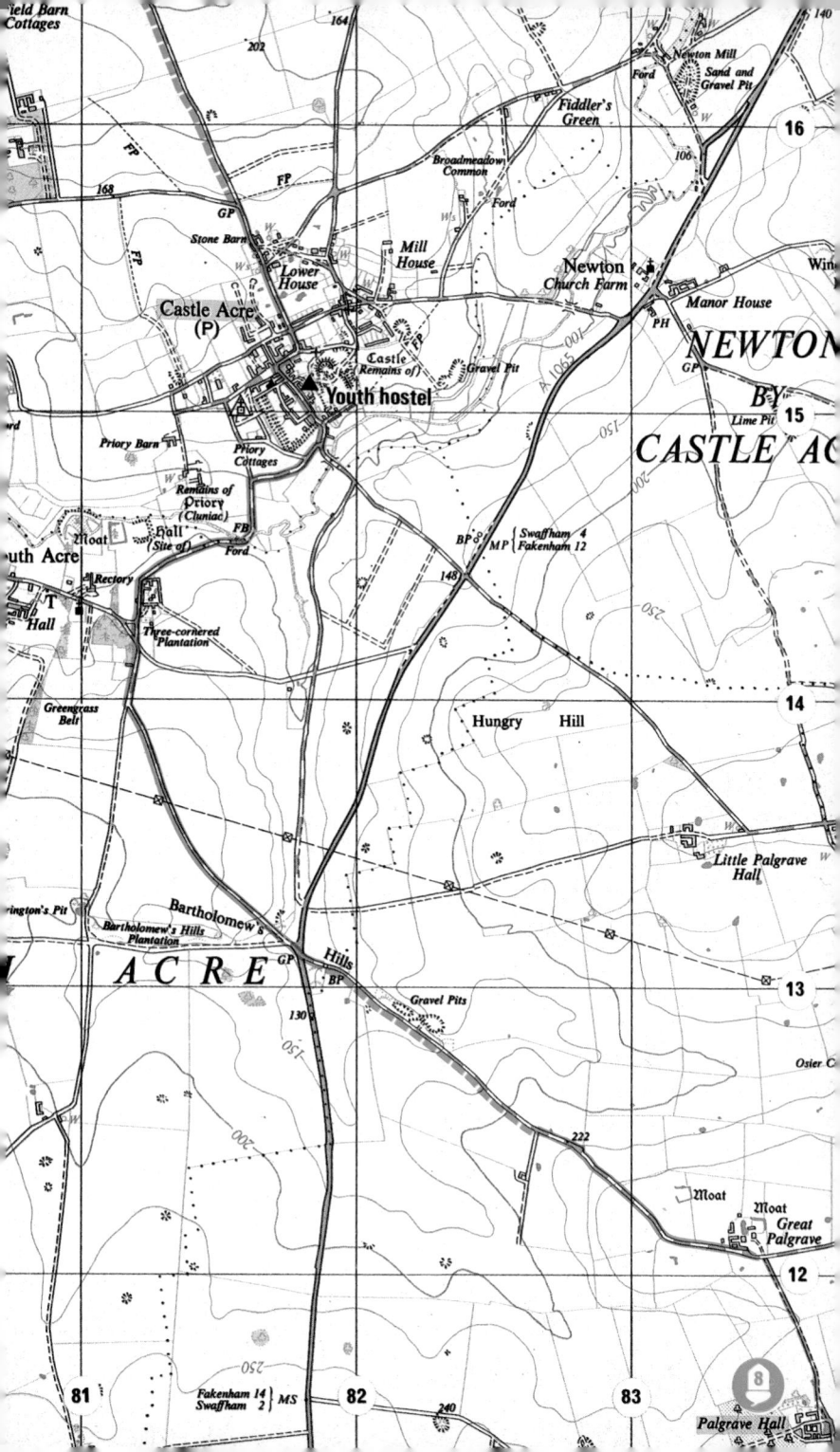

Castle Acre to Holme-next-the-Sea

33 kilometres (20 miles)

This is the longest and most straightforward of the Peddars Way stretches for, once clear of Castle Acre, the old road continues in a persistent line for most of the way to the coast. Much of the route from Castle Acre to Ringstead, other than the first 5 kilometres, is by grassy, stony track, though there are some short metalled sections. It is on this stretch that the character of the walk changes again, now moving through agricultural and then coastal landscapes. Ringstead, about 28 kilometres away, is the next community of any size touched by the LDR.

Leave **Castle Acre** by the green and turn left on to the Great Massingham road. Keep to the pavement as far as possible.

A few minutes' walk away, just past Stone Barn, a newly created footpath runs behind the hedge parallel with the road enabling the walker to keep away from the traffic. Look for the waymark on the west side of the road at a point where a farm road runs towards Manor House. The new footpath runs along the edge of the fields until it reaches the cross-roads near Old Wicken Farm, where the route joins the road again.

For most of the way this is a gradual uphill climb until, some 5 kilometres from Castle Acre, **Shepherd's Bush** (a name omitted from some maps) is reached.

Do remember to stay on the verge where possible on the road section, and keep in single file.

The plantation-fringed Breckland landscapes are now far behind. Instead, vistas begin to open out, and horizons expand. Farming dominates the countryside once more as the path leads towards the 'uplands' of Norfolk. The theoretical line of the Icknield Way runs roughly parallel with the Peddars Way about 5 kilometres to the west, and many of the fields beyond Shepherd's Bush are divided by tracks, boundaries and belts of trees which ribbon backwards and forwards between the two.

At Shepherd's Bush the Massingham road swings away to the right while the Peddars Way, maintaining its inevitable direction, reverts to the appearance of a grassy farm track.

Great
Massingham

Fring Cross

Those with time to spare might care to visit the pretty villages of **Great and Little Massingham**. Otherwise, and for most of the next long stretch to Fring Cross, the Peddars Way becomes increasingly remote, moving through an area of wide skies, open fields and occasional farm vehicles. In some places sections of hedgerows have survived the modern blitz. In other places there have been losses, and farm fields press close on both sides of the track. Particularly in summer it sometimes seems that the only things moving are rabbits and skylarks.

As for the Peddars Way, its surface varies from short sections of metalling to lengths of stony track, and for a few metres it has the appearance of a terrace, the land falling away gently to the east. But in the main it has an uneven and sometimes rutted and eroded top. It is easy, pleasant walking.

Pipeline installation

The path dips again shortly before the A148 at Harpley Dams and in quick succession passes, on the right, a pipeline installation (the short white 'hurdles' seen beside the path and in neighbouring fields are underground pipeline markers, not stiles) and on the left the former crossing-keeper's house alongside the disused Heacham–Wells railway trackbed. The line was opened in 1866 to connect with the successful King's Lynn–Hunstanton route which began its commercial life four years earlier. It finally 'ran out of steam' in 1953.

Have a care when crossing the A148, for the road is wide and relatively modern and in consequence the traffic moves quickly.

Over the road there is a short, sharp climb towards Harpley Common. The tree-fringed outline of the Houghton estate can be seen to the east while ahead, on the opposite side of the track, is **Anmer**, a village associated with the Sandringham Royal estate.

Sandringham House itself is about 8 kilometres to the west and can be reached by turning left at the junction with the Anmer-Harpley road. Beside these crossroads, and in neighbouring fields, a number of Bronze Age barrows are visible. Most are now relatively small and one or two are simply marked by clumps of trees and bushes. So too are some of the many marl pits (there are said to be 50 on either side of the Peddars Way between Harpley Dams and Anmer), the creations of the 18th century agricultural 'improvers'.

Just over the crossroads is another curiosity, an area known as Anmer Minque. The original meaning is lost but it is thought to refer to broken, stony or bumpy ground, a meaning familiar to seamen, perhaps, who recall the dangerous reef near the Channel Islands known as *Les Minquiers*.

Some of the sections along the next few kilometres sometimes become overgrown and thus quite damp in wet weather, or with heavy dew. But there are compensations. There are some fine views, particularly to the east, while one section has lush verges and high hedges on both sides.

The line of the Roman road coincides with a parish boundary here, and it is interesting that the Peddars Way seems to

The Peddars Way near Harpley Dams

67

have retained much of its considerable width. The stretch which passes to the west of Bircham is a green and attractive area, quiet and isolated, and yet well known to strollers. During fine weather it is not unusual to see families walking or enjoying picnics on the grass.

Further on the majestic outline of Bircham windmill, a Norfolk corn mill (with seasonal opening to the public), is visible to the east.

After climbing much of the way from Anmer the path levels out and offers wide views, as though pausing prior to the descent to **Fring Cross** at the crossing point of the Sedgeford–Fring road. Here, as the path drops towards the old ford, where once there was a wayside cross, the Peddars Way is wide and grassy and there is lush greenery. Sedgeford beckons from the west, but if you pause at the top of the final stretch to the road, and look ahead towards the distant hill, you will see the line of the Roman road marked by a long hedgerow snaking across the fields and disappearing over the brow.

The water element in the ford is provided by the Heacham river which feeds Sedgeford and trickles on towards Fring. At the point where it crosses the Peddars Way it is usually little more than a pond, and in summer is sometimes completely dry. Care should be exercised, though, for the approach to the footbridge can be wet and muddy.

Not far from Sedgeford a remarkable Iron Age torc made

Cottages at Sedgeford

Landscape near Fring

of electrum, an alloy of gold and silver, was found in the 1960s. Now in the British Museum it provides evidence of the wealth and talents of some sections of the north-west Norfolk community in the first century BC. Further to the west, on the outskirts of Heacham, is Caley Mill, the home of Norfolk Lavender. Lavender is grown at Heacham, Choseley and the Queen's Sandringham estate, and nearly one-third goes for export.

The magazine

Over the Fring road the path climbs the hill to the right of the hedgeline. Shortly after passing Dovehill Wood it changes to the other side of the hedge and then turns left and right towards the hamlet of Littleport, which is near the site of the largely forgotten medieval village of Gnatingdon. The path runs close to a row of cottages and then meets the Sedgeford-Docking road. Turn right (towards Docking) and then almost immediately left beside the somewhat unusual **Sedgeford Magazine** house.

The magazine is thought to have been built by Sir Hamon le Strange about 1640 as a magazine or armoury where muster weapons and powder for the Smithdon Hundred could be stored. Royalist weapons were reputedly kept there, too.

Later, the path passes Magazine Farm and crosses the former Heacham–Wells railway line. The metals have gone and it is now little more than a farm track. Pass over and follow the hedge to a T-junction; turn left and then right towards a distant shelter belt, pass the edge of it, and descend into **Ringstead**. The track here has all the appearance of a green lane.

Once the crossroads is reached the route bears west and
then north through the village to link with the main road to
Holme. On the other side of the village there is a right and
left turn.

Ringstead is an interesting village with a mellow and stony
texture. To the west is Ringstead Downs, an unusual (for
Norfolk) chalkland valley, which is also the last known
seaward termination of the Icknield Way. To the east is
Courtyard Farm, farmed by conservationist and Labour peer,
Lord Melchett. A former president of the Ramblers'
Association he has dedicated new rights of way on his land
and established wildlife habitats there.

It is possible that a branch of the Peddars Way swung
north-west towards Old Hunstanton. There were originally
two churches in the village. One, dedicated to St. Peter, is in
ruins. The present church, St. Andrew's, was begun in the
14th century and substantially restored in 1865. In passing,
as it were, the Gin Trap public house has an interesting
collection of rural memorabilia.

Once clear of Ringstead and on the way to Holme glimpses
of the sea become frequent, even though it is still 4 kilometres away. The Wash can sometimes be seen to the west
while the remains of the Ringstead mill provide a prominent
landmark close to the path. A short distance beyond the mill
the route turns sharp left (opposite a bungalow), leaving the
main road behind. It follows a field boundary and then turns
right to pick up the true line of the Peddars Way again,
marked here by a line of bushes.

Now the sea begins to dominate the horizon.

In Ringstead, incidentally, the main road is wrongly signposted as the Peddars Way. The 'new' section of the LDR is a more accurate representation of the original line.

Follow the field boundary and cross the road (Old Hunstanton–Thornham) with care.

If you wish to visit the seaward termination at **Holme** continue northwards along Seagate, a metalled road, towards the car park and beach. The original terminus of the Peddars Way is not known. Today, it simply peters out on the wide beach amid the dunes.

Walkers wishing to visit Hunstanton can pick up the line of the Norfolk Coast Path at the bridge on the west side of the road leading to the beach.

Either way, the walker who began the journey at Knettishall Heath has now covered about 75 kilometres (46 miles) and has arrived in the village of Holme-next-the-Sea, one of the most populous places on the entire length of the Norfolk stretch of the Peddars Way.

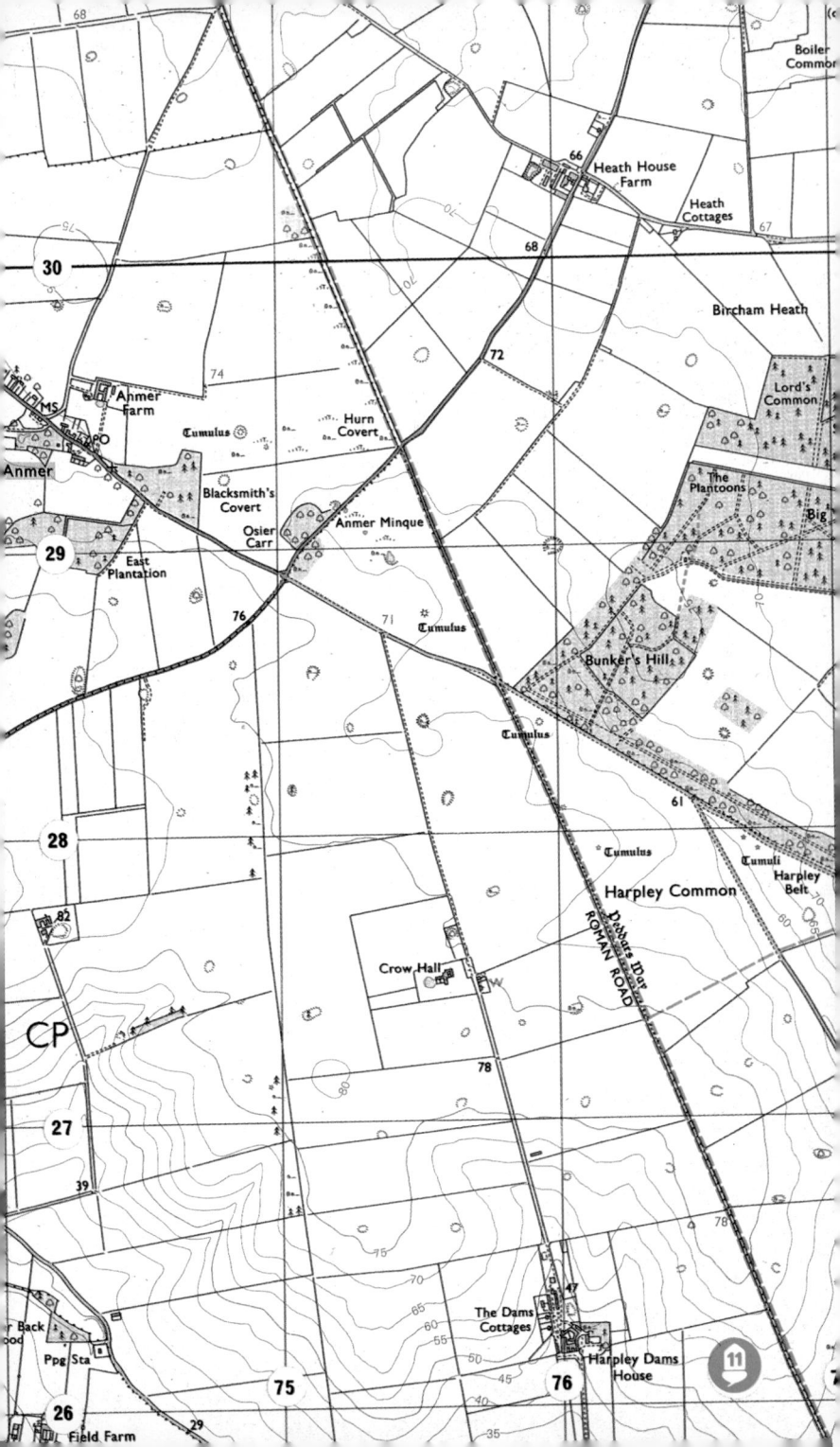

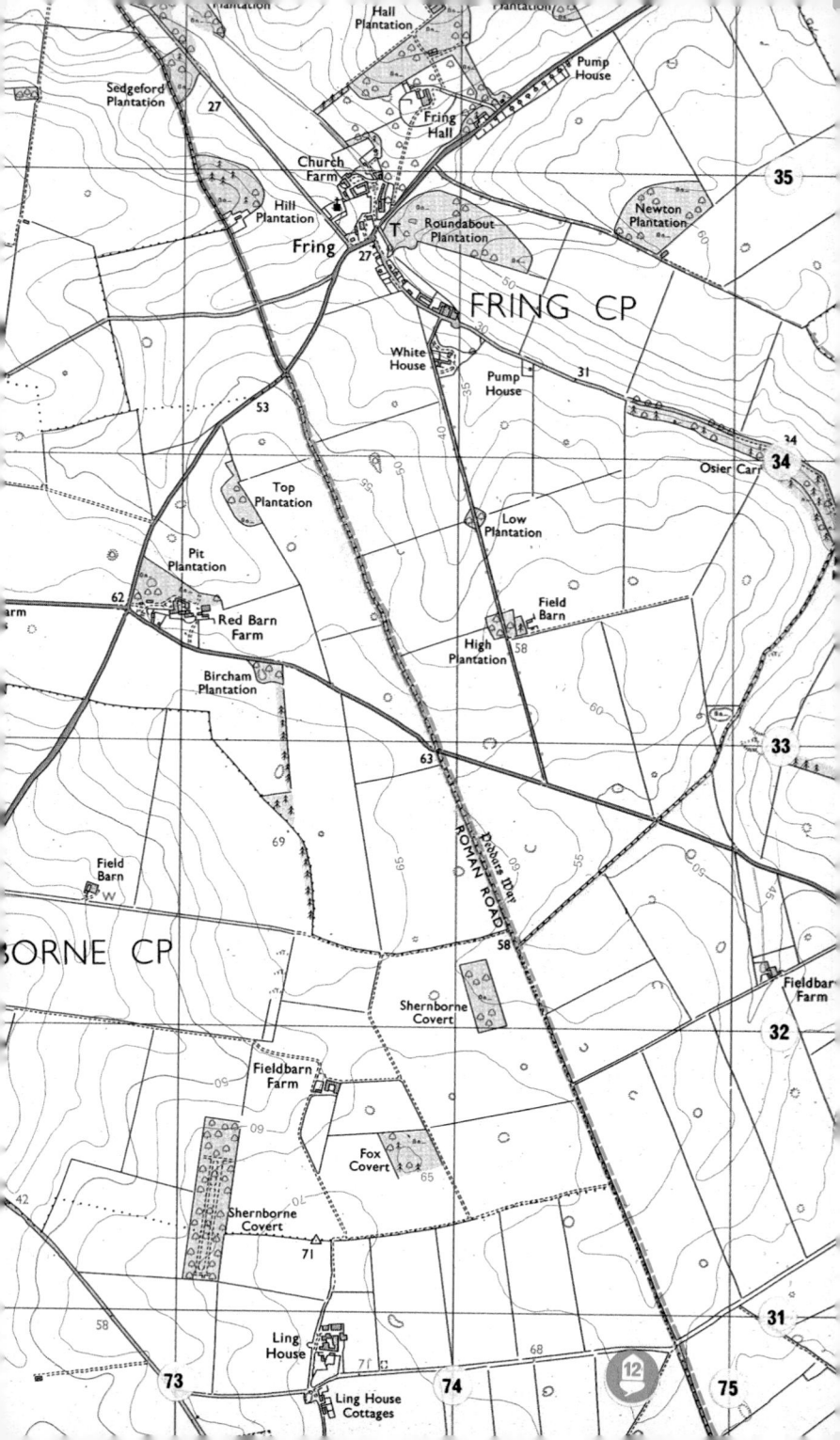

Norfolk
Coast Path
continued on
map 16

Gore Point

Broad Water

44

P

Beach
Cottage

Springs

6 Spr

HOLME NEXT THE SEA

Holme
House

11

FB

13

14

16

16

15

Sch

Holme next the Sea

Sea Gate

Kirkgate

Thurlow
Cottage

28

W

Vicarage

King's

43

Norfolk
Coast Path
continued on
map 15

Manor House

M S

King's Lynn 18

BS

GP

40

GP

33

The
Pool

Spr

Field Barn

Windpump

79

Long
Plantation

Windpump

Half Moon
Plantation

King's Lynn 17

Gipsy Green

North Belt

Birthday
Wood

Green Bank

Iron Age Founder's Hoard
found AD 1950

42

FB

Hunstanton
Hall

Deodara
Wood

The
Octagon

Ilex
Wood

FB

Kimberley
Plantation

lding's
Pit

Mill Farm

Windmill
(Disused)

W

BS

Ash

Oak

Stone

The
Scratch

127

Field Barn

NTON

nton Park

Oak

Stone

Anglo-Saxon
Burial Ground

Green Broom
Plantation

Hob's Mount

GP

GP

41

Grove

BS

Elms
Thorn
Oak Ash
Beech

Half Moon
Plantation

Gedding's
Farm

95

Bluestone Farm

Blues
Pl

Ringstead Lodge

School

er's
tion

Spring Meadow
Pits

BS

P

Rhos Ard

Ringstead

Inn

East End
Farm

53

Burnham Road
Farm

SL

14

70

Glebe Farm

d

49

50

72

Field
Barn

Elms
Apple Tree
Elm

Hall Farm

St. Peter's Church

RINGSTE

Hunstanton to Brancaster

17 kilometres (10 miles)

This first section of the Coast Path is a nice study in contrasts. The route follows a clifftop path at Hunstanton—from which the Lincolnshire coast on the far side of the Wash is sometimes in sight—provides a bracing stretch of dune walking, an inland route through isolated farmland, and finishes on the edge of the salt-marshes at Brancaster. In historical terms it passes a salubrious Victorian watering place, the area of a prehistoric forest, continues through a former port, and ends not far from the site of a Roman shore fort.

As its name suggests **Old Hunstanton** is the original part of the town. After the railway line arrived in the 1860s however, the Le Strange family developed a largely new site as a resort, and thus Hunstanton gained its distinctive face through the liberal use of gingery carstone. It is the only East Anglian resort to face west, which gives it a constantly breezy countenance.

Alas, the railway line has gone, but the clifftop hotels remain and there is a modern leisure centre and a magnificent beach. The cliffs are worth looking at from the aspect of the beach, too, for they are a striped sandwich of layers of white chalk, red limestone and carstone.

Begin the walk on the central green, opposite the old entrance to the former pier (the last vestiges of which were swept away in the 1970s) and follow the road past the ornamental gardens to the path along the top of the cliffs.

The restless Wash dominates the view and you can often see sandbanks, and on the far side on a clear day, not only the Lincolnshire coast but also the faint outline of Boston's church, known as the Stump. There might also be a glimpse of a jet fighter far out and low over the sea heading towards the Holbeach bombing range in Lincolnshire, or an air-sea rescue helicopter on patrol. Sea, wind and cliff dominate, however, and it is interesting that the Royal National Lifeboat Institute, which had a rowing lifeboat here in 1867, selected Hunstanton in 1920 for the first testing of the caterpillar tractor lifeboat launch system.

The ruins of St. Edmund's Chapel and Hunstanton's old lighthouse are soon reached. The chapel is thought to be a

Fulmar

Great skua

Black-headed gull

Spear thistle

Mallow

Thrift

Wheatear

Alexanders

13th-century building erected on the very spot, some say, where Edmund landed from northern Europe in the 9th century. No one has ever explained why the martyr-king should have come ashore at the foot of towering cliffs when he could have had an easier landfall a little further along the coast; but it is a passing thought. This corner of the cliffs retains the name St. Edmund's Point to this day, and its importance as a seaman's landmark is emphasised by the former lighthouse (built 1830, though not the first on this site) and by its current use as a coastguard marine rescue observation point. From here a close watch can be kept on shipping in the Wash.

Pick up the cliff-edge path just beyond the car park. The cliffs themselves begin to peter out but they afford a good view of the curving coastline ahead before they do. At the end of the car park take a somewhat indistinct path in the north-west corner down to the beach.

There is a brief walk on a footpath by the dunes until a beach access road is seen on the right. Turn here and walk up the slope until the Le Strange Arms Hotel is immediately ahead. Then, at the junction, turn sharp left on to an unevenly surfaced lane. Pass the golf clubhouse on the left and follow the road until it swings right near Warren Farm. On the left at the corner is a gate leading on to the golf course. Go through the gate and pick up the LDR along the edge of the links beside a small stream.

There is, incidentally, an interesting piece of local folklore about the Le Strange family. It relates that at some point in its history the family was given lands which included the seaward side 'out to the Wash itself, as far as a man on horseback, at low tide, could ride, then throw a javelin . . .'

Golf greens and tees occasionally close in on the LDR path but there is ample room for walkers and golfers providing everyone observes the usual rules of etiquette. The walking is easy and pleasant, and the route becomes increasingly distinct. The last few metres of the path leave the links behind and run momentarily alongside a caravan site. Turn left when the path joins the road beside the bridge, and head towards the beach.

Remains of St. Edmund's Chapel, Hunstanton

Holme-next-the-Sea is a popular place, particularly in summer; this road, and the adjacent car park, can become choked with traffic and visitors.

Turning the corner

Holme is also the last known termination of the Peddars Way. The Icknield Way fades out in this vicinity, too, and just outside the village is Green Bank, where an Iron Age hoard was discovered. A suggestion has been made that a grid-like pattern of fields and roads basically to the south and the east of Holme may represent the surviving remnants of a Roman land-settlement scheme for retired soldiers and settlers.

The village also represents the place where the LDR theoretically leaves the Wash and 'turns the corner' to face the north-west and north Norfolk coastline.

On the landward side of the dunes, however, turn right on to a sandy track by Holme Dunes nature reserve (see Wildlife and nature reserves). It is also waymarked as a Heritage Coast walk. Here the path runs along a boardwalk beside pools and sea lavender marsh and becomes increasingly lonely as the sandy headland of Gore Point is approached.

There is an invigorating feeling of isolation here, and long panoramas of sandy bank, wide sky and thundering surf can be seen on the nearby beach. It can be a hard walk on soft sand, but there are many compensations. There can also be a sad amount of tidal debris, much of it maritime rubbish, and sometimes the occasional dead seal can be seen on the beach.

Holme Dunes
nature reserve

Thornham

The black patches visible on the sand are some of the remains of the ancient forest of the North Sea basin, mighty trees now reduced to clumps of a wet peaty substance.

Once Broad Water corner is reached the LDR finally leaves the beach through convenient gaps in the bank and adopts a raised status on top of a sea defence bank heading roughly south. After a zigzag the path moves alongside Thornham Creek and crosses part of it by an old bridge.

The final stretch to the village, which branches east and is marked by a Footpath sign, can be difficult in that lengths of it are sometimes overgrown. Eventually a lane is reached which runs south to **Thornham**, a trim village of stone, brick and flint houses topped with red pantile roofs, graced by an interesting church and serviced by three old and venerated pubs, the King's Head, the Chequers, and the Lifeboat, where you can indulge in the 'ancient' art of 'gnurdling', which involves throwing discs into a hole in a pub seat.

Thornham, as a port, formerly had granaries and jetties and a useful trade in timber, oil cake, malt and coal, but it lost out to the railway when the line to Hunstanton opened. Instead, it turned its attention to iron working, and the business started in a small way in 1887. By 1899 Thornham had five smiths and between 15 and 24 people employed at forges turning out ornamental work which received wide recognition and Royal patronage. The original works closed in 1920.

Shady lane near
Brancaster

Inland detour

There is no suitable seaward route east of Thornham so the
LDR makes a brief inland incursion here. Follow the main
road through the village and turn right on to the lane signposted to Choseley. There is a steady climb up a straight,
narrow road for nearly 2 kilometres before a small triangular
clump of trees is reached.

This countryside is extensively farmed and despite views of
the sea and the coast there is a feeling of emptiness about the
landscape. Choseley, indeed, is thinly populated, and as a
parish it is also unusual in that it has no church. To the west
is Beacon Hill, once thought to have been a Roman signal
station but now known to have had a far more complex
history. Excavation of the site showed Neolithic and Bronze
Age occupation, a fortlet dating to the time of the Boudican
revolt, and a 6th- and 7th-century cemetery. The whole of the
Choseley area seems to have been heavily Romanised.

Turn east along the northern edge of the plantation, keeping the hedgeline on your left, and continue along the side
of the fields for about 500 metres to a wide farm road. The
LDR crosses this lonely landscape along a broad grassy line
(in places reminiscent of the Peddars Way), and two roads
leading to Titchwell, then turns towards the distant sea
again and approaches **Brancaster** along a pleasant country
lane.

Once in the village cross over the junction of the main
road, walk past St. Mary's church on the road to the beach,
and after 300 metres turn right on to a footpath running
along the southern edge of the Brancaster salt-marsh. This

can be a very wet and muddy environment, but a timber walkway has been laid over the worst sections.

Titchwell Marsh bird reserve (see Wildlife and nature reserves) is about 2 kilometres to the west at this point, while the Brancaster course of the Royal West Norfolk Golf Club is seaward of the saltings.

After about 1 kilometre, incidentally, the marsh footpath runs parallel with Rack Hill, just to the south, site of the 4th-century Saxon shore fort known as Branodunum. Alas, the ruins were extensively quarried about 1770, but the site, which has been acquired by the National Trust, is now open to the public and direct access can be obtained from the Coast Path. Aerial photographs show that Branodunum was very extensive, embracing a fortified area and civilian settlements. The Dalmation Cavalry was garrisoned here, presumably charged with the task of helping to protect this corner of the Roman empire from incursions and raids.

The last anchorage

Peddars Way
continued from
map 14.

P

16

Golf Links

F B

HOLME NEXT THE SEA

*Beach
Cottage*

Springs

*Holme
House*

Sea Gate

Vicarage

Kirkgate

*Thurlow
Cottage*

Holme next the Sea

King's Lynn 18

M. 71

House

B S

G P

G P

King's Lynn 19

N S

G P

*The Drove
House*

*Plug
Pits*

F Bs

Manor

Gore Point

Breakwaters

Broad Water

Saltings

Saltings

W E S T

S A N D S

Low Water Mark of Ordinary Tides

B P

B P

P

HARBOUR

68

43

44

45

69

71

72

50

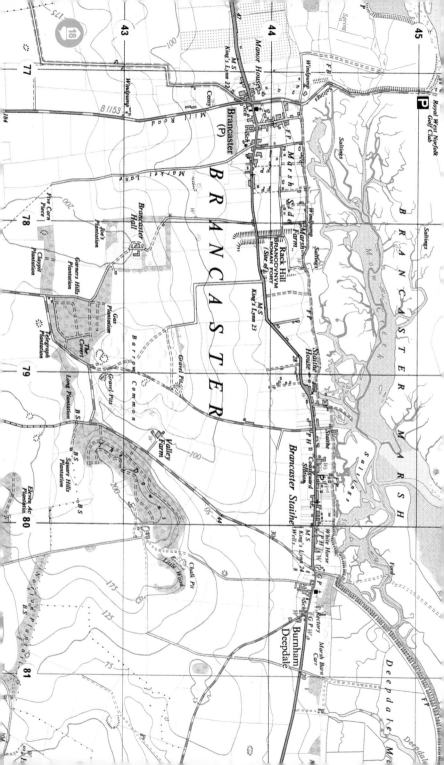

Brancaster to Wells-next-the-Sea

19 kilometres (12½ miles)

The second stage of the Coast Path incorporates a route across grassy embankments and a wide, sandy bay, followed by a tree-fringed path along the edge of grazing meadows leading to the port of Wells. If Brancaster can be described as the gateway to 'Nelson country' then this section of the LDR embraces the bulk of it, including a clutch of the famous Burnham villages.

The walk along the edge of **Brancaster** saltings continues beyond Rack Hill and Staithe House, the wettest parts of the path being crossed by stout timber walkways. The masts of boats moored at Brancaster Staithe glisten in the distance, and reeds whisper in the wind.

This section requires care because of its unevenness and the ever present possibility of soggy or watery conditions underfoot, but the going does improve at the stile. Turn left beyond the houses and then right by the creeks and pick up the LDR again in the gap between two fishermen's sheds. Follow the path along the edges of the creeks as far as the sea bank.

Brancaster Staithe once had a regular sea trade in coal and grain and, in 1841, six master mariners are said to have lived here. Earlier still the Staithe is believed to have had one of the largest malthouses in the country. Now the village is almost hemmed in by saltings, but it remains a busy and pretty leisure sailing centre with many boats moored in the creeks. From here you can book passage to Scolt Head, though a visit does require a permit.

Shellfish were brought ashore in this area in Roman times and the Staithe is one of the places along the Norfolk coast where the industry still survives. The crab and lobster fishermen of Cromer and Sheringham, and some whelk boats, constitute some of the other elements; but here it is mussels.

Young mussels (called seed) are collected from breeding grounds in the Wash and transplanted in 'lays' in the Brancaster creeks to be left up to three years to grow. They are then sorted, riddled and washed overnight in cleansing pools before being transported to London or the Midlands.

Traditional grazing

Before the LDR moves on to the top of the bank it passes

91

Saxon round
tower of
Burnham
Deepdale church

some cleansing pools, and mussel fishermen can sometimes be seen working on their boats and equipment.

The wide sweep of the sea bank stretches towards Scolt Head, Norton Creek and Gun Hill once you have climbed to the top and put Brancaster Staithe behind. The path along the bank is difficult in places, sometimes being choked with long grass and thistles. This is an extraordinary world of birds and creeks, wind and sky. The further along the bank so the silence seems to increase. Here the views are spectacular, and the sound of a distant aircraft comes as an intrusion into privacy.

After a long walk along this breezy dividing line between creek and marsh the bank swings south-east and then south-west towards Burnham Norton. A cross bank enables the walker to turn east again over the river Burn in sight of Overy windmill. Then the LDR crosses a field and turns left to run parallel with the A149 road into **Burnham Overy Staithe.** Turn left at the crossroads into West Harbour Way.

The quay is the essence of Overy Staithe, a tidy village with moored boats and the continual noise of wire stays slapping on masts. Another formerly flourishing port it was able to make the transition to an agricultural village when the railways came. Overy's public house, incidentally, is called The Hero, and there is no doubt at all who he could have been.

It is said there were once seven Burnham villages, though only five properly survive: Deepdale (its Saxon round tower church has an unusual font depicting the seasons of the year), Norton, Market (where 18th-century houses face each other across the green), Overy and Thorpe.

The hero

Horatio Nelson was born at Burnham Thorpe in 1758 at or near the Rectory (the original was demolished in 1803) on the road to Creake. His father the rector, though not a rich man, nevertheless managed to send the boy to school in Norwich and North Walsham and perhaps Downham Market. In 1771 he joined HMS *Raisonable.* Seven years later he returned to Burnham Thorpe with his new wife, Fanny, to live in semi-retirement for a number of years. In 1793, however, he was appointed Captain of the *Agamemnon*, taking a number of Norfolk men with him and, by the time he landed at Great Yarmouth in 1800 with Sir William and Lady Hamilton, he was already a hero. His carriage was pulled through the

Waiting for the tide

| Sand couch grass | Lyme grass | Marram grass | Cord grass | Salt-marsh (sea-meadow grass) |

streets by the cheering crowds. Ten years after Nelson's death, and following the death of her mother, daughter Horatia returned to stay with Nelson's sister, Susannah, at Burnham Market, and later married the curate there.

There is a story that Nelson learned to sail on local waters. Perhaps he did. In any event there are Nelson memorabilia to be seen, and on Trafalgar Day (21 October) the church of Burnham Thorpe flies the white ensign, a replica of that flown from the *Victory* at Trafalgar.

On the sea bank beyond Overy Staithe there is some good walking alongside the saltings all the way to Gun Hill. The dunes suddenly loom large and there is an undulating climb over the top and then down to the beach on the seaward side.

Do keep to existing tracks among the dunes to minimise the possibility of erosion. In May, June and July walkers may be directed away from one section of the beach. There is a colony of nesting terns here in an area which is usually indicated by temporary fences, posts and appeals to 'keep out'.

Holkham is a marvellous bay and there is now about 4 kilometres of walking over flat sand across its broad

expanse. The tide retreats a great distance, but it is worth remembering that it also returns at considerable speed, too. It is a good idea, if the sand is dry and the walking hard, to look for slightly wetter and marginally firmer surfaces closer to the high water line. In this way it is sometimes possible to find partial relief for aching limbs.

The bay is a popular spot on warm days but, because of its size, it rarely conveys an impression of being crowded. The belts of pines to landward, on Holkham Meals, were planted about 1860 to prevent the dunes moving further inland and so that the marshes could be reclaimed. Holkham Camp earthworks, a little further to the south, is thought to have been an Iron Age fort. Not far away a Roman road once ran south towards Tofttrees. Much of the area is a national nature reserve managed by the Nature Conservancy Council, and it is necessary to keep to the footpaths. Holkham estate, including the Hall, is also close at hand and well worth a trip down Lady Ann's Road.

To continue the LDR, however, follow the curve of the bay towards Lady Ann's Road, which is the main access point for the beach and car park. There is a boardwalk over the loose sand. Go through the gate and, before reaching the car park, turn immediately sharp left on to the path behind the trees.

This sheltered section provides easy and comfortable walking, the trees sometimes giving relief from boisterous sea breezes. In fact, the smell of the pines, the sandy surfaces, and clumps of rosebay willowherb along the verges give it something of the atmosphere of Breckland.

Long horizons

Terns

Curlew

Marram grass

Grayling

Common tern

Marsh hellebore

Sea holly

Hound's tongue

Sea bindweed

Sea spurge

Sea sandwort

Sea campion

Common blue

Sea rocket

97

Busy port

In most places the path is dusty, grassy and unusually quiet. Closer to Wells there are likely to be more strollers and more paths striking off through the trees towards the beach. In the event the LDR finally passes a boating lake—all that remains of the former fishing boat haven—a caravan site and car park and comes out on to the beach road not far from the lifeboat station. The path is on top of the bank which now runs for about 1.6 kilometres straight to **Wells-next-the-Sea**. During the summer part of the distance to Wells quay is covered by a narrow gauge railway. Turn left and walk along the quay.

Wells is now the only port on the north Norfolk coast with a usable harbour, but it is still limited in terms of access and capacity. Nevertheless, in 1981/2 it had its busiest year for a century, a record number of ships docking with animal feed, soya, fish meal, potash and potatoes. Nearly all Britain's whelks come across Wells Bar, too. The town has a small fleet.

For many years the prosperity of Wells has been tied to the sea and to agriculture. Wells fishermen once sailed far and wide, local shipwrights built brigs, schooners and sloops, and the harbour and narrow streets were filled with the sights and sounds of cargo handlers, ropemakers, sailmakers, carters, blockmakers and chandlers. In the early 1800s Wells was the chief port between King's Lynn and Yarmouth, handling 300 vessels a year.

The agricultural prosperity of the area, brought about by the pioneering work of the Holkham and Raynham estates, provided a further means of expansion. In 1857, however, the Wells and Fakenham railway line was opened, and the decline of the port began.

Awaiting
unloading

Pines near to the beach at Wells

Wells' beach, fringed by pines, beach huts and the lifeboat house, is wide and popular, and the quay and town are often busy with visitors. The harbour front is dominated by warehouses and a gantry, and it is a sobering thought that the gales of 1978 were fierce enough to lift a coaster and dump it on top of the quay.

Other reminders of the dangerous qualities of the sea are close at hand. The town was badly pounded by the floods of 1953, the effects of which also killed many of the trees at Abraham's Bosom, the former haven which is a noted beauty spot. In 1880, 11 men of Wells perished when the lifeboat capsized on its way to a grounded ship.

In 1879, following a violent storm, the church of St. Nicholas was gutted by fire after the Wells and Holkham fire engines and crew had toiled to try to curb the blaze. It was later rebuilt. John Fryer, one of the officers of the mutiny

Beach huts at
Holme

ship, HMS *Bounty*, is buried in the churchyard, while the
death in 1779 of the master of the 'floating light', one of the
first East Coast lightships, is recorded there.

In the town is a grassed area surrounded by trees known
as the Buttlands, which has been used for fairs and may at
one time have been an archery ground.

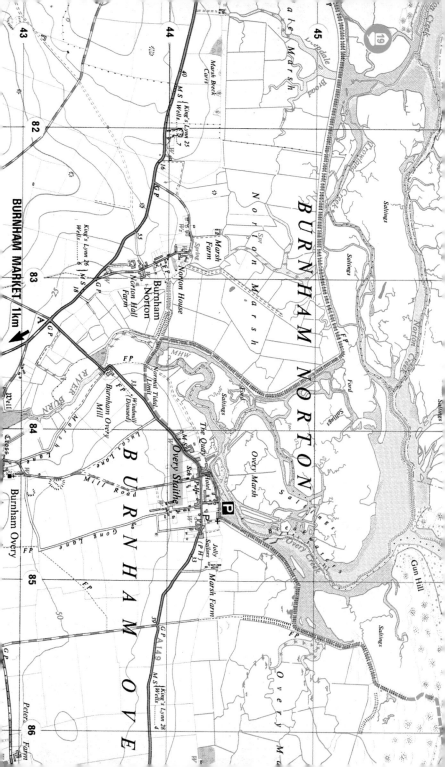

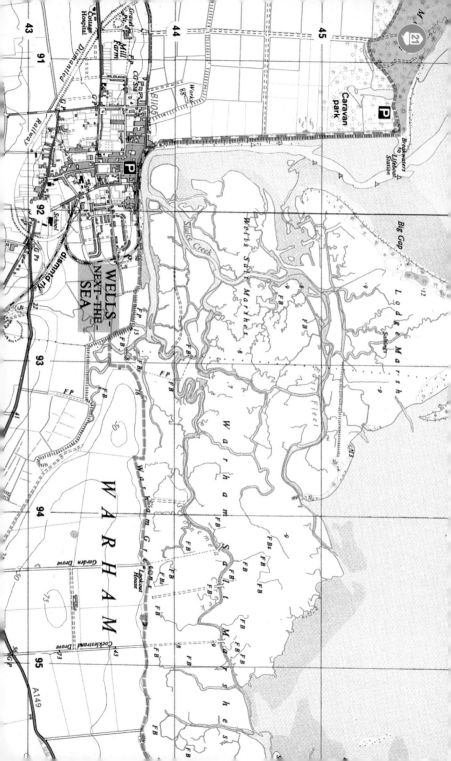

Wells-next-the-Sea to Cley-next-the-Sea

17 kilometres (10½ miles)

Shipping and the sea have had a major influence on the landscape of the third section of the Coast Path, for the LDR now takes in lonely salt-marshes and sea defence and drainage banks. It also passes a number of villages with former maritime connections. Blakeney and Cley, and their inland neighbour, Wiveton, were once busy and important seaports with extensive trading connections. Blakeney is now a popular leisure sailing centre while the other two have largely lost their commercial links with the sea.

Walk along **Wells** quay past the Custom House, the ancient Golden Fleece pub, Jolly Sailors' Yard, and another pub, the Shipwright's Arms. Just beyond a slipway, where the road divides, take the left fork and shortly after climb up on the sea defence bank. About 550 metres from the start of the bank it turns right, and 300 metres later, sharp left. The path then turns left again and plunges into dense undergrowth.

Though overgrown in parts the route is nevertheless quite distinct and it emerges, moments later, into more open country on the fringes of the marshes.

The stretch across Warham marshes can be wet and muddy and the walker is strongly advised to stay on the path. The creeks and rivulets can flood at high tide. The going does eventually become easier, and the path finally evolves into a broad grassy swathe dominated to the north by the flat marshes and the sound of birds and the far off sea. In July and August violet-blue flowers of sea lavender tinge the landscape. Nearly 5 kilometres to the south is Warham Camp, an Iron Age fort with massive banks and ditches built into a nook of the river Stiffkey.

Once the LDR crosses the road between Stiffkey and the marshes the route then joins a partially metalled track.

Stiffkey is famous for its cockles, called Stewkey Blues, which were gathered by the women of the village. The fishery started to decline in the 1950s and has now almost died out.

It is also remembered for a famous scandal of the 1930s involving the Rev. Harold Davidson. Deprived of his living for spending much time in Soho, Davidson became known as

Blakeney quay

the 'prostitutes' parson'. He embarked on a campaign to clear his name which involved appearing in music hall, sitting in a barrel on Blackpool's Golden Mile and in a lion's cage at Skegness. He died after being mauled by a lion. His former Rectory is a fine detached two-storey house set back from the road in the village. Henry Williamson, author of *Tarka the Otter*, lived in Stiffkey during the Second World War.

The path continues unevenly and stubbornly towards Morston, sometimes grassed and sometimes not, passing many creeks. It rises on to a bank to skirt Freshes Creek and then turns the corner and levels out again along Morston Greens. Blakeney Point (see Wildlife and nature reserves) is visible to the north, while clusters of masts bristle ahead and Blakeney church, with its characteristic towers, begins to dominate the background as it will do, by degrees, most of the way to Sheringham.

Once **Morston** is reached turn left towards the harbour, which is invariably busy with boats, and then right on to the sea bank beside Morston Creek.

Morston is connected to Blakeney harbour by a narrow tidal creek. A ferry runs from the village to Blakeney Point, and that salty delicacy, samphire, can be found in the vicinity, too. Bait digging for lugworms is another local 'industry', as it is at Blakeney and Stiffkey.

The path along the top of the bank is sometimes uneven and the greenery high; but the walking is good alongside Agar Creek, and the masts of boats moored at **Blakeney** soon come into view. Then it loops past Red House and finally reaches the quay. Follow the road along the quay to the car park and take the path on top of the sea bank on the far side. Alongside the quay is the channel, deep at high tide but almost dry when the tide is out.

Blakeney is a village—dedicated to leisure—packed in summer with people and boats, and full of 'second homes'. Houses and buildings overlook the quay and the boats, and crowd together in yards off the High Street. This stretch of the coast was once the 'gateway to England' for a surprising variety of goods and cargoes, though as a port Blakeney eventually lost some of its importance to Cley, on the other side of the channel of the river Glaven. The three villages—Blakeney, Cley and Wiveton, which is further inland—all carry tell-tale signs of former maritime importance.

Blakeney's history is considerable. In 1329 it sent a vessel and provisions to Dublin to transport troops to Scotland, and in 1347 Blakeney ships were present at the siege of Calais. By the 16th century its vessels were ranging as far as Iceland, and when the Armada threatened, Blakeney, Cley and Wiveton between them mustered 36 ships. There may have been boat building here, too. There was certainly smuggling, and a general fear of the lonely creeks was fuelled by local legends of 'Shuck', a black ghost dog, and 'hytersprites' on the marshes.

Clearly, Blakeney haven was very important in shipping terms, though it is now more usually flooded with leisure sailors and trippers, some of whom make the short trip across to Blakeney Point. It is interesting that in the 17th century the area hereabouts produced three men destined to become Admirals—Sir Christopher Myngs, of Salthouse, Sir John Narborough, of Cockthorpe, and Sir Cloudesley Shovell, also of Cockthorpe.

Blakeney's 15th-century church contains several memor-

No sailing today

ials which testify to the community's seagoing past, including one stone in the churchyard, dated 1881, which reads:

'I with seven others went
Our fellow men to save
A heavy wave upset our boat
We met a watery grave'.

One famous name in the churchyard is that of Sir Henry 'Tim' Birkin, the racing driver. Sportsman and pilot, he was best known as one of the 'Bentley Boys' of the late 1920s and early 1930s. Birkin's racing career lasted six years, during which time he had many Grand Prix successes. Although he never lived at Blakeney, Sir Henry spent many holidays there. He died in 1953.

The church is also interesting in that it has a small second tower at the north-east corner of the chancel. The church's main tower is fairly lofty, and a substantial local landmark. The second tower, it is thought, may have been a beacon and a guide to shipping. Right or wrong, the fact remains that Blakeney's towers provide a distinctive outline visible for many miles.

A village called Snitterley once lay off Blakeney, but it was

The quiet marsh

Off the beaten
track

lost because of coastal changes. Something similar happened
at Cromer where the hamlet of Shipden finally toppled as the
cliffs receded between the 14th and 17th centuries.

Maritime past

Wiveton, about 2 kilometres inland from Blakeney, also has
an interesting maritime past, a handsome church, a late
medieval bridge, a huge ironbound 'charity chest', and a
legend. This relates to Raulf Greneway who (according to the
story) was a foundling discovered on the village green. Other
research suggests he was the son of a Wiveton merchant and
shipowner who became an alderman of London and in 1558
made a charitable bequest which still benefits residents and
the church.

Heading north along the sea bank, and then north-east as
it swings towards Blakeney Eye, there are marvellous views
of Blakeney, Cley with its distinctive windmill, Blakeney
Point, and a real feeling of windswept isolation. Incidentally,
do not contemplate walking across the saltings to the Point.
Cley channel can produce some difficult problems when the
tide begins to turn.

At its extreme point, and before the bank turns away from
the sea towards Cley, the indistinct outline of the ruins of the

13th-century Blakeney chapel can be glimpsed in the fields.
It may also have served as a beacon or landmark for shipping.
There may be cattle grazing in the vicinity. Walkers are
asked not to feed them, and to make sure no plastic bags or
debris are left in the area.

Once over the stile and having turned right the path on its
lofty bank heads unerringly towards **Cley** (sometimes pronounced 'Cly') and its mill. Again, there are fine views. The
final stretch to the village runs on top of the bank by the side
of the Blakeney–Cley road; but shortly before it ends the
path drops to the road and enters the village by a T-junction.
Turn left into a narrow street (beware of traffic at this point
as the pavement is limited) and turn left again down a narrow
passage shortly after passing Rocket House. Turn right at
the end of the passage and follow the path by the old quay
wall all the way to Cley mill.

Cley, on the east side of the Glaven channel and now
separated from the sea by marshland, was a flourishing
fishing and trading port. The church, built in 1250 and rebuilt
in the 14th century, reflects this importance. Calthorpe's
Bank, built in the first half of the 17th century, allowed ships
to use Cley quay but began to obstruct navigation to
Wiveton. The marshes were steadily reclaimed during the
17th and 18th centuries, but the creeks and river had already
begun to silt up. Wiveton ceased to trade as a port, and by
1855 Cley's port was in decline. The Customs and Excise
office closed in 1853. Smuggling at Blakeney and Cley, as an
organised activity, died out a little later.

Saltings near
Cley

Cley is now the centre of much bird-watching activity, and it lures many enthusiasts, the main attractions being the Norfolk Naturalists' Trust's Cley Marsh bird reserve (see Wildlife and nature reserves) and the Dick Bagnall-Oakley Memorial Centre, also run by the Trust.

The windmill was built about 1819 and is now restored and open to the public.

Cley-next-the-Sea to Cromer

22 kilometres (13½ miles)

Some of the quiet scenes along this final length of the LDR are in direct contrast to its busy coastal past. This is one of the most varied sections of the route for it incorporates a long stretch of shingle shore, a fine walk along breezy clifftops, and an attractive inland route. It also takes the walker to the popular resorts of Sheringham and Cromer.

Walk past the front of **Cley** mill and follow the path on the grassy bank by the saltings, reed and grazing marshes, and on towards the sea-shore. Turn right on the beach on the seaward side of the shingle bank. There is now a long and sometimes hard walk all the way to Weybourne Hope.

The shingle bank is an integral part of the coastal defence system. Do not walk on top of it as this can cause damage. Swimming is not recommended in this vicinity, either. The currents are very dangerous.

Walking on shingle can be tiring, but wide skies and the crashing sea—and exquisite vegetation such as sea holly and the yellow-horned poppy—are major compensations. After about 1½ kilometres the route crosses over the bank and continues along the landward side where the going is easier and more sheltered. The stretch alongside the bird reserve —marked by a wire fence, and out of bounds—can sometimes be wet and boggy. Inland of the LDR is the extensive Salthouse Broad.

The curiously named Cley Eye, Little Eye and Flat Eye, and landward, Gramborough Hill itself, are hillocks much eroded by the sea. They may have been connected with the salt-making industry for which this neighbourhood was famous. Roman remains have also been found in the area, and Warborough Hill may have been a signal station.

Salthouse faces marshes which since the 17th century have spread to silt up the port and cut the village off from the sea. Salthouse church has some interesting carved graffiti in the chancel which is said to represent vessels of the 16th to the 19th centuries. The main road marks the former shore.

The village was a collecting depot for salt made here from sea-water which was used, among other things, for preserving fish caught by the boats of Salthouse, Blakeney, Cley and

ey mill

115

Wiveton. It provided extensive trade over a very long period, and it is thought there was a salt warehouse here as early as the 11th century. Sarbury Hill, to the west of the village, is called Salt Hill on a map of 1649.

The sea defences of this area have been breached many times, most recently in the massive North Sea surge of January, 1953, when many properties were damaged and one person was drowned.

One interesting character from the locality was a certain Onesiphorus Randall who was born in Cley in 1798 and evidently made his fortune in London. He returned and built a spectacular castle-like folly on Salthouse beach, which was known first as Randall's Folly and then as Rocket House. It was subsequently used by coastguards, as a private house, as a military look-out, and as a holiday home. It, too, was badly damaged by the 1953 floods, and later demolished.

Military associations with the area have survived the centuries. Deep water close inshore has bred one invasion scare after another, and elaborate defences were planned by Elizabeth I to combat the possibility of invasion by Spain. These plans included the destruction of crops and bridges and the flooding of the marshes.

The basic vulnerability of the area also gave birth to the jingle:

'He who would old England win
Must at Weybourne Hope begin'.

Military interest survives to this day.

During both world wars troops were stationed here along with gun emplacements, defensive positions and during

The cliffs near
Weybourne

Waiting for
the cod

World War Two, an anti-aircraft practice firing range. As the LDR takes on a more hilly aspect during its approach to Weybourne the walker will notice the fences around the old Ministry of Defence property overlooking the sea. RAF Weybourne is now the home of a mobile radar unit, an annex to RAF Neatishead. Ever-turning radar heads scan the coastal skies for 24 hours a day.

The coastguard service and volunteers have dealt with many wrecks and a great deal of smuggling. In 1837 troopers engaged an armed gang on the beach and after a battle in which two men were wounded they recovered 240 gallons of brandy. Local tradition says millers set their windmill sails in the form of a cross to warn the smugglers of danger. In 1858 submarine telegraph cables from Borkum, Germany, were brought ashore here, and in 1950 a cable link with Esbjerg, Denmark, was laid.

Sea anglers
At **Weybourne** the shingle finally disappears and the cliffs slowly take over. The shelving beach, a major attraction for sea anglers, remains too dangerous for swimming.

Climb the path leading up the cliffs and head towards Sher-

Approaching
Sheringham

ingham. The views are very fine, with a rolling farming landscape to the south (and perhaps a glimpse of a passing steam train on the Sheringham–Weybourne line), and to the north the thundering surf and the sight of ships perhaps heading into or out of Yarmouth Roads.

It should be remembered that in this vicinity the cliffs are subject to constant erosion and in a continually weakening condition. Resist a temptation to observe the fulmars at close range and stay away from the cliff edge. Always be alert to the possibility of cliff falls.

At Water Hill, not far from Weybourne windmill, the path turns momentarily inland to skirt a wall and house, and then returns to the cliffside. Continue past the golf course and climb the steep Skelding Hill to the coastguard lookout. **Sheringham** is now spread below, nestling between its twin hills. To the west the coastline and in consequence a long section of the LDR curves away into the misty distance.

Walk down into the town and along Sheringham promenade to a series of cliff steps beside some public conveniences. This is the way to Beeston Hill.

Sheringham is a jolly patchwork of holiday trade and local industry. Once upon a time it had an agricultural community at Upper Sheringham and a fishing community closer to the sea. There is no natural harbour, so boats are hauled up on the beach. Sheringham is also famous for fish, lobsters, crabs and whelks, its lifeboat station—and a liking for family nicknames such as 'Downtide', 'Joyful' and 'Paris'. The local crab-pots were invented in about 1862 and are still much the same today.

Residents born in Sheringham of Sheringham-born parents qualify to be known as Shannocks. The origin of the name is

118

not known, but some claim (though rarely publicly) that it derives from 'shanny', a dialect word meaning unruly, which suggests it may relate to periods of rivalry with Cromer fishermen. True or not, Shannock is a name proudly carried.

It is the sea which is often unruly now, and the promenade is sometimes wet with spray. However, follow the steep path to the top of Beeston Hill and pause to catch your breath and study the view beside the Ordnance Survey triangulation point on the summit. Ahead are the Runton villages, and beyond them, Cromer church.

Behind is Sheringham and in the far distance, when visibility is good, a final glimpse of the distinctive outline of Blakeney church's two towers. Continue down the path until it turns sharp right by a hedge and passes over a railway crossing. Turn left at the road then cross over on to the old road and turn right on to a gravelled track by some farm buildings leading to Beeston Hall.

As the path approaches the National Trust's property at Roman Camp the scenery changes again. The soil is light and there are birch trees and bracken. A smell of pine permeates the glades.

Before leaving the coast, the freshwater deposits of the Cromer Forest Bed are of considerable geological interest. So-called because of the fossilised wood they contain, the deposits were formed in the delta of a river, possibly the Rhine. The geological series appears intermittently in the cliffs from Weybourne to Kessingland. Many plants such as oak, ash, hazel, lime, hornbeam, alder and pine have been

Sheringham
station

identified from pollen, and the bones and teeth of southern elephant, hippopotamus, Etruscan rhinoceros, hyena and deer have been found.

Turn half left at Stone Hill and follow the sandy track through the greenery towards Roman Camp. Away from the coastal breeze—though there are continual glimpses of the sea between the trees—it can be quite warm in the woods. Pass the caravan site and cafeteria, cross over the road, and then turn left on to a rough track which descends towards a camp site.

Highest point
The crest of Beacon Hill, topped by a radio mast and near the point where the track begins, is the highest point in Norfolk, clocking up a modest 105 metres (346 feet). Roman Camp itself, which has no real connection with the Romans, may take its name from the site of a beacon and telegraph station. It is a substantial area of heathland dotted with shallow pits, and there is evidence of Saxo-Norman-medieval iron smelting.

At the entrance to the camp site turn right on to the narrow path which skirts its boundary. It crosses the fields towards Manor Farm and continues with some good walking along a shady track under a railway viaduct. Cromer church soon comes into view again. When the path joins a metalled road, and then a main road, turn towards Cromer and walk directly to the town.

Cromer is a famous resort known for its crabs, which are sent all over the country, for picturesque boats hauled on to

The Cromer
lifeboat in action

Cromer

the beach, its lifeboat station and pier. It was once a fashionable watering place, a product, like Hunstanton, of the railway age. It has fishermen's cottages and narrow streets, a fine beach, deck-chairs and beach huts, and a lighthouse on the cliffs. There are many hints of a former gentility. The dominant landmark, in the town and surrounding countryside, is the 15th-century church of St. Peter and St. Paul. At 160 feet its magnificent tower is the highest in Norfolk.

The RNLI took over the lifeboat in 1857, and it was a front line station during the Second World War when its two boats were credited with the rescue of 450 people. Cromer's most famous local hero is Henry Blogg, who died in 1954. Blogg was cox for more than 50 years and he was nationally famous for many brave exploits and for having been awarded the RNLI gold medal three times, the silver medal four times, the George Cross and the British Empire Medal. He and his crews saved 873 lives during his span of service. His memorial describes him as 'one of the bravest men who ever lived'. In 1970 another Cromer lifeboatman, Henry 'Shrimp' Davies, was also awarded the BEM.

In 1883 a visitor to the area was Clement Scott, a London journalist and theatre critic, who later wrote an article in *The Daily Telegraph* extolling the quiet and colourful virtues of 'Poppyland'. The locality subsequently became the gathering place of writers and poets, and a 'Poppyland' industry developed. A stone trough at the junction of the Overstand – Northrepps road acts as a memorial to Scott.

Modern herbicides have put paid to the bulk of the poppies. Nevertheless, splashes of brilliant red can sometimes be seen against the background of fields and a shining sea.

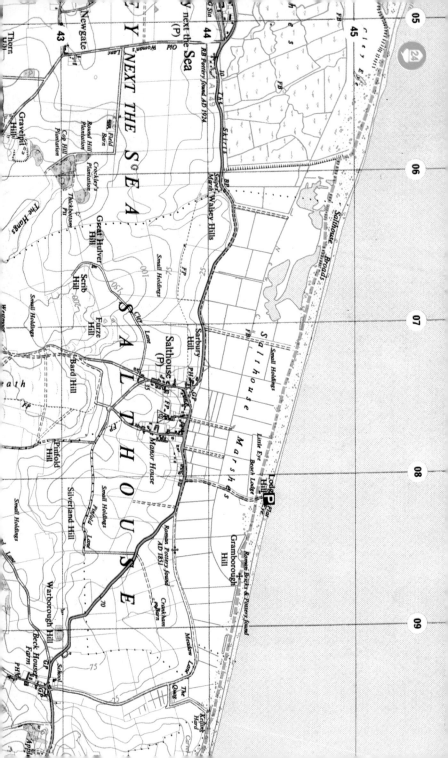

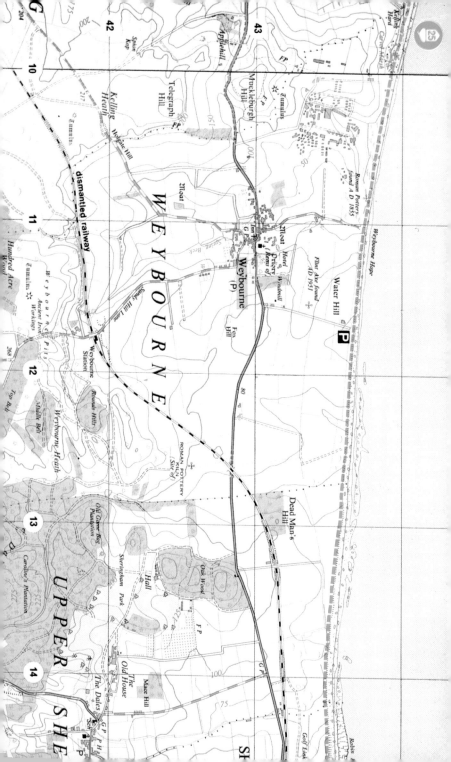

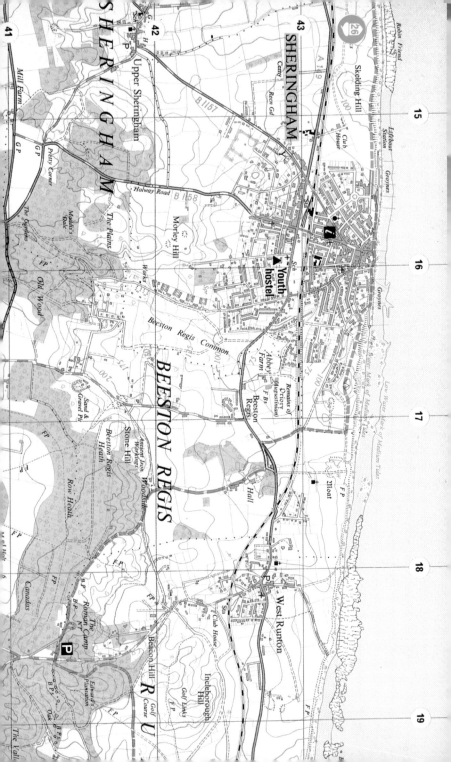

Additional walks

A growth of interest in recreational walking—particularly during the last decade—has stimulated the creation of a number of localised routes, long and short, and in some cases the publication of descriptive leaflets and guided walks programmes. In addition to the LDR, therefore, a number of other paths in the area are available.

In the south, for example, there is a 38-kilometre (24-mile) forest path from West Stow, in Suffolk, to Didlington High Ash, which passes through Santon Downham and close to Grimes Graves, mainly through Forestry Commission plantations. A forest map and general information leaflets are available from the Forestry Commission.

At Swaffham a 9-kilometre (6-mile) circular route known as Swaefas Way has been devised by Breckland District Council, with financial assistance from the Countryside Commission, which incorporates part of the Peddars Way. Walkers on the Way can visit Swaffham by turning off the LDR (Swaefas Way is waymarked) at Dalton's Plantation (Procession Way) or at the Sporle–Swaffham road. A leaflet about Swaefas Way is available from Breckland District Council.

Norfolk's Heritage Coast stretches from Holme-next-the-Sea to Weybourne and sets of leaflets describing circular walks are on sale. Walks are also available in Holkham Park and at Courtyard Farm, Ringstead; and there are Town Trails in Thetford and Wells and parish walks in Watton and Castle Acre.

A much longer available route is a link from Cromer to Great Yarmouth, known as Weavers' Way, which passes through or by Felbrigg, Blickling, Aylsham, North Walsham, Stalham and Acle. The combined length of Weavers' Way and the long distance path (in other words, Knettishall Heath to Great Yarmouth via Holme and Cromer) is about 217 kilometres (135 miles).

Literature about all these walks is available from the Planning and Property Department of Norfolk County Council. A publications list will be sent in return for a stamped addressed envelope.

Longer term possibilities under consideration include a Wash Coast route stretching from the Lincolnshire border to the mouth of the Great Ouse river; a Waveney Way route from Great Yarmouth to the Peddars Way at Knettishall; and an Icknield Way route which would link with the Peddars Way and Norfolk Coast Path.

Nearby places of interest

The countryside surrounding the Peddars Way and Norfolk Coast Path is full of sites, landscapes, towns and villages well worth visiting. Those who want to stray from the path to enjoy some of them ought to obtain a copy of the East Anglia Tourist Board's *East Anglian Guide*, published annually, which gives relevant opening dates and times. Details are also available from the tourist information centres at Norwich, Thetford, King's Lynn and Hunstanton; the seasonal centres at Cromer, Sheringham and Little Walsingham; the seasonal information point at Wells; and from some district councils.

Here is a brief personal selection of some places of interest within 20 kilometres (12 miles) of the route. It does not, of course, include Norwich which is worth a book on its own.

Brandon Country Park About 12 hectares (32 acres) of the former grounds of Brandon Park House, with woodland, a lake, picnic areas, walks and a visitor centre.

Castle Rising The village hints at past importance, but it is difficult to visualise that Roman and Norman ships may once have entered the estuary of the Babingley river. The sea has since receded some 6 kilometres or so, the haven having probably ceased to function in the Middle Ages.

There is a certain mischievous glee, therefore, in the old rhyme:

> 'Rising was a seaport when Lynn was but a marsh.
> Now King's Lynn it is a seaport town, and Rising fares the worse'.

The description 'seaport' is an exaggeration, but Castle Rising does still have much to commend it. Carstone walls give the place a nicely textured surface. Trinity Hospital Almshouses (founded c. 1614 for women 'of honest life and conversation, religious, grave and discreet, able to read . . . to be 56 years of age at least, no common beggar, harlot, scold, drunkard, haunter of taverns, inns and alehouses') provide the occasional spectacle of the ladies going to church

Holkham church

129

wearing the traditional red cloak and black hat. Rising's crowning glory, however, is the Norman castle built by William d'Albini. For a time it was a Royal residence, for Queen Isabella once lived there.

East Harling East Harling sits astride the known route of a Roman road which once wound its way from Ixworth towards Attleborough; but it is a semi-isolated community in the sense that its through-route importance is largely superseded by the main A11 trunk road. As a result it has retained much of its shape and atmosphere, serving as a quiet half-way house between the afforested plantations to the west and mid-Norfolk communities to the north and east.

Its church, partly rebuilt in 1449, has a particularly fine short spire (similar to St. Peter Mancroft, Norwich) and contains two important 15th-century monuments.

Grimes Graves An eerie place in many respects; a 13-hectare (34-acre) stretch of heath bounded by plantations and pitted by a mass of bumps and hollows. Grim, incidentally, was the Norse name for Odin.

The site was long thought to be an ancient fortification or

Grimes Graves Neolithic flint mine with flint axes and arrowheads from Norfolk

Holkham Hall

village, and its true significance was not realised until 1869–70 when the Rev. Canon Greenwell excavated a depression to a depth of 9 metres (32 feet). It was identified as an old flint mine shaft which had become filled in. In fact, more than 350 have now been identified, which means the area is pockmarked with shafts and honeycombed with inter-connecting galleries.

These flint mines relate to the Late Neolithic and vary from opencast pits to 12-metre shafts with linking galleries. They had been sunk through chalk and overlying sand, and the complex may have employed specialist bands of flint knappers and miners who used deer antlers as picks. It is esti-mated that more than 50,000 shed antlers were used in this dangerous work, which presupposes not only plentiful deer in the vicinity but also sufficient people to gather them. One antler still carries the chalky fingerprint of a miner.

It is a chilling and thought-provoking experience to clatter down the DoE-installed ladder to the floor of the shaft, which is open to the public, to feel the cold air and see the tunnels and the marks of Neolithic miners' picks.

Holkham Thomas Coke, 1st Earl of Leicester, began build-ing Holkham Hall in 1734 after William Kent had prepared the drawings. In 1776 the estate descended to Thomas William Coke, otherwise 'Coke of Norfolk', one of the great 'improving landlords' of the 18th and 19th centuries.

He enlarged the park and applied a four-course rotation to his home farms, imposing it on his many tenants on the 20,235-hectare (50,000-acre) estate. He also experimented with newly emerging breeds of sheep, cattle and pigs, and caused tenants to marl their light soils (with dressings of clay mixed with chalk), thus helping to produce many of the marl pits of north Norfolk.

The Palladian hall houses vast collections of paintings, tapestries, statues and furnishings. There is also a Bygones museum collection. The large park, landscaped by Capability Brown, is one of the finest in the region.

Houghton The largest country house in Norfolk, it was built for Sir Robert Walpole, the first Prime Minister of England, early in the 18th century. The village of Houghton, evidently thought to be too close to the site, was demolished and rebuilt to the south, to become New Houghton. The Hall itself is enormous and ornate, and many of the original furnishings by William Kent remain in the State rooms.

There is also a collection of about 20,000 model soldiers and other militaria, and formal gardens. Houghton is now the home of the Cholmondeley family.

King's Lynn The borough retains a flavour of old England, a whiff of ships, trade and the Hanseatic League, but the new is beginning to catch up with the old. Modern shopping precincts and the Tuesday and Saturday markets clamour for custom, and the streets are busy with traffic. Lynn entertained King John before he set off on his ill-fated journey across the Wash marshes, where he is said to have lost his baggage en route for Newark; and Captain George Vancouver, the sailor-explorer, was born here.

The Custom House, King's Lynn

132

Much of Lynn's history is tied to its river and port, a safe deep-water anchorage sheltered from the unpredictable Wash, and narrow streets run down to quays where merchants' houses and warehouses presented an aspect of wealth. There are a number of important buildings, including two guild halls. Lynn is also the home of a nationally famous festival of music and the arts. For all that, it is not a show town for tourists, being much too busy to concentrate wholly on a single theme. As Lynn fishermen search the Wash for shrimps and shellfish, so the port is slowly redeveloping trade with a number of traditional markets.

Sandringham A private estate owned by the Royal family and one of the homes of Her Majesty the Queen.

The estate was purchased in 1862 by Edward, Prince of Wales, who had the old house demolished and the present one built of car and Ketton stone. The grounds and museum are sometimes open to the public, but it is essential to check opening dates and times. There is a large country park with lawns and gardens, a nature trail and a museum of motor cars. The estate church is nearby.

Security arrangements are unobtrusive and there is a local tradition, if the Royal family are in residence, of leaving them alone—even if they are seen out riding.

Santon Downham A forestry village, a small island in a sea of green, approached by narrow tree-lined roads. Oddly, it lies at the heart of the former East Anglian 'desert' which comprised windswept heaths grazed bare by over-abundant

133

rabbits. In the 17th century the village was almost buried by
a sandstorm, and the Little Ouse river blocked. The arrival
of the Forestry Commission and the creation of plantations
in the 1920s has helped to stabilise the 'travelling sands' but
folk memories live on. There is one apocryphal tale, with a
number of variations, in which a farmer hereabouts is asked
if his land is in Norfolk or Suffolk (the river, of course, being
the county boundary). 'Well, sir,' he explains, 'sometimes it's
in one and sometimes in the other. It blows back and forth.'

Santon is a delightful backwater with a uniquely restful
atmosphere. The little Norman church and rushy river are
nearby, and there are walks and picnic spots. Foresters'
houses ring a central green and the Commission's district
office and information centre (with car park) are readily
available. Nearby, too, are the nurseries where young coni-
fers are reared.

Steam railways The Wells and Walsingham Light Railway
runs an 8-mile return journey along the old Great Eastern
trackbed. Based in Wells it is believed to be the longest
$10\frac{1}{4}$-inch-gauge railway in Britain. The North Norfolk Railway runs steam trains, in season, from Sheringham to
Weybourne. There are historic locomotives and rolling stock.
Full details from The Station, Sheringham.

Swaffham In the late 18th century this was a fashionable
centre, with balls, theatre and soirées. It was known as the
'Montpellier of England'. Some of the elegant houses and

large buildings remain. Swaffham's hare coursing club was formed in 1776 to course the surrounding heaths.

Now it is the centre of an agricultural area. There is a busy Saturday market, a wide and impressive market place, a memorable church, and a legend. John Chapman, the Swaffham pedlar, dreamed that if he went to London Bridge he could learn something to his advantage. He did, and there met another man who said he had dreamed of a chest of money under a tree in Swaffham. The pedlar returned home, found his fortune, and built the north aisle of the church.

Thetford The name, Thetford, has been interpreted as the 'people's ford', or 'the ford everybody uses', and there is no doubt it has been an important crossing point for centuries. The huge earthworks at Castle Hill and the general line of the Icknield Way suggest a pre-Roman importance. In the 9th century marauding Danes were prone to sack it, rebuild it, and then over-winter hereabouts.

In the 11th century it was an important town with its own

The Gate House, Thetford Priory

Crown copyright. Reproduced with permission of the controller of HMSO.

mint, and was for a time the seat of the East Anglian bishopric. Thomas Paine (author of *The Rights of Man*, *The Age of Reason*, etc) was born here, and there is a statue to him in the town. It is now a busy mixture of old and new, ranging from the Castle mound, museum and Priory ruins to a riverside shopping centre and fringe estates embracing new industries and an increasing population, including many from the London area. In many ways it is the capital of Breckland and the gateway to Norfolk. The forest is never very far away.

The Walsinghams Great and Little Walsingham comprised an important monastic centre in the Middle Ages. Before the Dissolution the Shrine of Our Lady of Walsingham had an international reputation and in this country was second in popularity only to Canterbury. Its visitors have included Erasmus (1511), Royalty, and the Archbishop of Canterbury (1980). The original shrine was built early in the 12th century. The Priory (established circa 1153) surrendered to the King in 1538 whereupon Walsingham ceased to be a pilgrim centre for 350 years.

A modern revival began in the 1890s and in 1934 pilgrims began arriving on a larger scale. The Roman Catholic and Anglican shrines are now visited by some 100,000 pilgrims a year. Here are many green and quiet lanes. It is a tranquil slice of the countryside.

West Stow A Suffolk country park with grassland, heathland, lake and river, and country walks; and a reconstructed Anglo-Saxon village with several complete buildings.

Accommodation

The creation of the route has lent considerable impetus to the provision of accommodation, which now ranges from hotels and bed and breakfast facilities to camp sites and hostels. In addition several bunk barns are planned along the route, including one at Ringstead which is likely to be in operation by the time the route is officially opened.

Some forms of accommodation are more difficult to find on the Peddars Way stretch of the path as the old road passes through areas of thinly-populated countryside and, in consequence, few villages. In some respects it is easier along the coastal section where communities have been catering for visitors for many years. All the same, tenting areas and other accommodation facilities are gradually being improved all along the LDR.

There is Youth Hostels Association provision at several centres including: King's Lynn and Brandon, which are in the general area of the LDR; and at Hunstanton and Sheringham, on the coastal section; while a further hostel at Castle Acre, which is conveniently half-way between Knettishall and Holme, is expected to open in 1985. There is also a hostel in Norwich, of course.

The Ramblers' Association and the Cyclists' Touring Club jointly produce a *Bed and Breakfast Guide*, and the Norfolk section includes accommodation in the area suitable for the LDR.

Information on all forms of accommodation, including camping and caravan sites, can also be obtained from East Anglia Tourist Board publications; from the Tourist Information Centre in Norwich; and from local (and sometimes seasonal) information centres at Bury St. Edmunds, Cromer, Hunstanton, King's Lynn, Sheringham and Thetford. Tourist information and publicity material is also available from North Norfolk District Council.

A further source of information is a guide regularly revised, published and sold by the Peddars Way Association. It also includes information relating to the Weavers Way extension. This guide gives current information on the whereabouts of camp sites, hostels, guest houses, and so on. It also indicates the location on the LDR of pubs, banks, shops, telephone kiosks and post offices.

Useful addresses

Countryside Commission
Eastern Regional Office
Terrington House
13–15 Hills Road
Cambridge CB2 1NL
Tel: Cambridge (0223) 354462

Norfolk County Council
County Hall
Martineau Lane
Norwich NR1 2DH
Tel: Norwich (0603) 611122

Suffolk County Council
St. Edmund House
Rope Walk
Ipswich IP4 1LZ
Tel: Ipswich (0473) 55801

Borough Council of King's Lynn and West Norfolk
King's Court
Chapel Street
King's Lynn PE30 1EX
Tel: King's Lynn (0553) 61241

North Norfolk District Council
Recreation & Amenities Dept.
Holt Road
Cromer NR27 9DZ
Tel: Cromer (0263) 513811

Breckland District Council
The Guildhall
East Dereham NR19 1EE
Tel: Dereham (0362) 5333

East Anglia Tourist Board
Toppesfield Hall
Hadleigh
Suffolk IP7 5DN
Tel: Hadleigh (0473) 822922

y village

Tourist Information Centre
Augustine Steward House
14 Tombland
Norwich NR3 1HF
Tel: Norwich (0603) 620679

British Rail
Travel Centre
Thorpe Station
Norwich NR1 1EF
Tel: Norwich (0603) 6320255

Eastern Counties Omnibus Company
Head Office
79 Thorpe Road
Norwich NR1 1UB
Tel: (0603) 620491

C.E. Petch & Son
High Street
Hopton IP22 2QX
Tel: Garboldisham (095 381) 228

The Ramblers' Association
1–5 Wandsworth Road
London SW8 2LJ
Tel: 01-582 6878

Peddars Way Association
150 Armes Street
Norwich NR2 4EG
Tel: Norwich (0603) 623070

Youth Hostels Association
Regional Office
40 Culver East Street
Colchester CO1 1DR
Tel: Colchester (0206) 44011

Nature Conservancy Council
Eastern Regional Office
60 Bracondale
Norwich NR1 2BE
Tel: Norwich (0603) 620558

Forestry Commission
District Office
Santon Downham
Brandon IP27 0TJ
Tel: Thetford (0842) 810271

National Trust
Regional Information Office
Blickling
Norwich NR11 6NF
Tel: Aylsham (0263) 733471

The Norfolk Naturalists' Trust
72 Cathedral Close
Norwich NR1 4DF
Tel: Norwich (0603) 625540

Royal Society for the Protection of Birds
East Anglian Office
Aldwych House
Bethel Street
Norwich NR2 1NR
Tel: Norwich (0603) 615920

Reading list

Some of the suggested titles listed here are available only through the libraries' service.

CAUTLEY, H. Munro. *Norfolk Churches*. Boydell 1979.

CHATWIN, C.P. *British Regional Geology: East Anglia and Adjoining Areas*. HMSO 1961.

CLARKE, Helen. *East Anglia*. Heinemann Education 1971.

CLARKE, R. Rainbird. *In Breckland Wilds*. EP Publishing 1974.

CLARKE, R. Rainbird. *East Anglia*. EP Publishing 1975.

COOK, Olive. *Breckland*. Hale 1980.

DYMOND, David. *The Norfolk Landscape*. Hodder and Stoughton 1985.

EDLIN, H.L. (editor for Forestry Commission). *East Anglian Forests*. HMSO 1972.

ELLIS, E.A. *Wild Flowers of the Coast*. Jarrold 1972.

FLETCHER, Ronald. *The East Anglians*. Patrick Stephens 1980.

KENNETT, David H. *Norfolk Villages*. Hale 1980.

MARGARY, Ivan D. *Roman Roads in Britain*. Baker 1973.

THE NORFOLK NATURALISTS' TRUST. *Nature in Norfolk*. Jarrold 1976.

PETCH, C.P. and SWANN, E.L. *Flora of Norfolk*. Jarrold 1968.

PEVSNER, Nikolaus. *North-East Norfolk and Norwich; and North-West and South Norfolk*. (Buildings of England series.) Penguin 1962.

RAVENSDALE, Jack and MUIR, Richard. *East Anglian Landscapes*. Michael Joseph 1984.

ROBINSON, Bruce. *Norfolk Origins 1: Hunters to First Farmers*. Acorn Editions 1981.

ROBINSON, Bruce and ROSE, Edwin J. *Norfolk Origins 2: Roads and Tracks*. Poppyland Publishing 1983.

SEAGO, M.J. *Birds of Norfolk*. Jarrold 1967.

SEYMOUR, John. *The Companion Guide to East Anglia*. Collins 1970.

SWANN, E.L. *Supplement to Flora of Norfolk*. Crowe 1975.

WADE MARTINS, Susanna. *A History of Norfolk*. Phillimore 1984.

WEBSTER, Graham. *Boudica*. Batsford 1978.

YAXLEY, David. *Portrait of Norfolk*. Hale 1977.

e beach
Cromer

COUNTRYSIDE ACCESS CHARTER

Countryside COMMISSION

YOUR RIGHTS OF WAY ARE

Ω Public footpaths – on foot only. *Sometimes waymarked in yellow*

Ω Bridleways – on foot, horseback and pedal cycle. *Sometimes waymarked in blue*

Ω Byways (usually old roads), most 'Roads Used as Public Paths' and, of course, public roads – all traffic. *Use maps, signs and waymarks. Ordnance Survey Pathfinder and Landranger maps show most public rights of way.*

ON RIGHTS OF WAY YOU CAN

Ω Take a pram, pushchair or wheelchair if practicable

Ω Take a dog (on a lead or under close control)

Ω Take a short route round an illegal obstruction or remove it sufficiently to get past.

YOU HAVE A RIGHT TO GO FOR RECREATION TO

Ω Public parks and open spaces – on foot

Ω Most commons near older towns and cities – on foot and sometimes on horseback

Ω Private land where the owner has a formal agreement with the local authority.

IN ADDITION you can *use* by local or established *custom or consent*, but ask for advice if you're unsure:

Ω Many areas of open country like moorland, fell and coastal areas, especially those of the National Trust, and some commons

Ω Some woods and forests, especially those owned by the Forestry Commission

Ω Country Parks and picnic sites

Ω Most beaches

Ω Canal towpaths

Ω Some private paths and tracks. *Consent sometimes extends to riding horses and pedal cycles.*

FOR YOUR INFORMATION

Ω County councils and London boroughs maintain and record rights of way, and register commons

Ω Obstructions, dangerous animals, harassment and misleading signs on rights of way are illegal and you should report them to the county council

Ω Paths across fields can be ploughed, but must normally be reinstated within two weeks

Ω Landowners can require you to leave land to which you have no right of access

Ω Motor vehicles are normally permitted only on roads, byways and some 'Roads Used as Public Paths'

Ω Follow any local bylaws.

**AND, WHEREVER YOU GO,
FOLLOW THE COUNTRY CODE**

Enjoy the countryside and respect its life and work

Guard against all risk of fire

Fasten all gates

Keep your dogs under close control

Keep to public paths across farmland

Use gates and stiles to cross fences, hedges and walls

Leave livestock, crops and machinery alone

Take your litter home

Help to keep all water clean

Protect wildlife, plants and trees

Take special care on country roads

Make no unnecessary noise.

This Charter is for practical guidance in England and Wales only. Fuller advice is given in a free booklet 'Out in the country' available from Countryside Commission Publications Despatch Department, 19-23 Albert Road, Manchester M19 2EQ.

Countryside
COMMISSION